"A book that establishes a truly wise, empathic, and motivating resonance with teens. It offers a straightforward and commonsensical way to deal with stress of all kinds and afflictive emotions and thoughts by inviting them into awareness and discovering that with a little mindfulness and heartfulness, *you* are much much bigger than they are!"

—**Jon Kabat-Zinn**, author of *Full Catastrophe Living* and *Wherever You Go, There You Are*

"Dzung Vo, my student, is a very dedicated and wonderful adolescent pediatrician. He has written this book as a record of experiences working with adolescents. It is a recommended book on mindfulness for teens and a teaching tool for the Wake Up Movement. I highly recommend this book for teens and teen educators."

—**Thich Nhat Hanh**, Zen Master, poet, scholar, activist, and author of *Being Peace*

"Dzung Vo has crafted an invaluable resource for teens everywhere. Inspiring teen voices, along with practical applications, make *The Mindful Teen* incredibly relevant and accessible. This heartfelt offering to the world is a *must-have* for teens, the parents of teens, and anyone who works with adolescents."

—**Meena Srinivasan**, author of *Teach, Breathe, Learn*

"This clear, simple book is not just for teens! Everyone can benefit from its profound, practical wisdom. I will recommend this to all the teens in my practice."

> —**Kathi Kemper, MD, MPH**, director of the Ohio State University Center for Integrative Health and Wellness, and author of *Mental Health, Naturally*

"This book can change your life, not because of anything it will convince you to do or believe, but because it offers you the tools to access your own wisdom, to calm yourself, and to find sensible solutions to the challenges you will face."

> —**Kenneth R. Ginsburg, MD**, author of *Building Resilience in Children and Teens*

"What teenager hasn't felt stressed, anxious, angry, or just plain unsettled? *The Mindful Teen* offers straightforward, understanding guidance for teens. Be yourself, find yourself, and create for yourself a lifelong ability to more easily manage the ups and downs of everyday life."

> —**Mark Bertin, MD**, developmental pediatrician and author of *Mindful Parenting for ADHD*

"*The Mindful Teen* is a beautifully written book that walks the line between making mindfulness easy and accessible to teens who may or may not be inclined to delve deeply into the topic and providing real substance and depth to a powerful practice and way of living. Full of understandable, doable practices, super relevant examples, and quotes, this book doesn't talk down to kids, but speaks up to future adults who deeply desire to overcome the challenges they face and not only succeed, but thrive: A valuable guide to living the practice of mindfulness that anyone could benefit from reading."

—**Steven D. Hickman, PsyD,** founder and executive director of the University of California, San Diego Center for Mindfulness, and associate clinical professor at the UC San Diego School of Medicine

"Despite the explosion of mindfulness literature in recent years, there are remarkably few high-quality mindfulness resources written specifically for adolescent populations. This gem of a book from Dzung Vo will go a long way in closing that gap. More than a series of techniques and exercises, *The Mindful Teen* provides the crucial contextual information necessary to answer the most important question teens have about mindfulness practice—*Why should I care about this?*"

—**Chris McKenna**, program director at Mindful Schools, http://www.mindfulschools.org

"A generous gift for the next generation. Dzung Vo offers adolescents a gentle path through a turbulent time, with skills they can use for the rest of their lives."

—**Christopher Willard, PsyD,** Cambridge Health Alliance/ Harvard Medical School, author of *Child's Mind* and *Mindfulness for Teen Anxiety*

"Dr. Vo provides intelligent and compassionate guidance toward mindfulness—a tool that can bring balance back into the increasingly imbalanced world of today's youth. As a psychiatrist, educator, and parent, I have been witness to the awesome effects of mindfulness firsthand. This book will change lives!"

—**Shimi Kang, MD**, psychiatrist and author of the national bestseller, *The Dolphin Way*

"If you are a teenager who wants to live a less stressful, more enjoyable life, I encourage you to read *The Mindful Teen*. This book offers powerful mindfulness exercises in a clear, simple, friendly, easy-to-use format. Start reading and experience the benefits, now."

—**Amy Saltzman, MD**, author of *A Still Quiet Place*

the *instant* help
solutions series

Young people today need mental health resources more than ever. That's why New Harbinger created the **Instant Help Solutions Series** especially for teens. Written by leading psychologists, physicians, and professionals, these evidence-based self-help books offer practical tips and strategies for dealing with a variety of mental health issues and life challenges teens face, such as depression, anxiety, bullying, eating disorders, trauma, and self-esteem problems.

Studies have shown that young people who learn healthy coping skills early on are better able to navigate problems later in life. Engaging and easy-to-use, these books provide teens with the tools they need to thrive—at home, at school, and on into adulthood.

This series is part of the **New Harbinger Instant Help Books** imprint, founded by renowned child psychologist Lawrence Shapiro. For a complete list of books in this series, visit newharbinger.com.

the
*mindful
teen

powerful skills to help you handle stress one moment at a time

DZUNG X. VO, MD, FAAP

Instant Help Books
An Imprint of New Harbinger Publications, Inc.

Distributed in Canada by Raincoast Books

Copyright © 2015 by Dzung X. Vo
            Instant Help
            An imprint of New Harbinger Publications, Inc.
            5674 Shattuck Avenue
            Oakland, CA 94609
            www.newharbinger.com

Cover design by Amy Shoup
Acquired by Tesilya Hanauer
Edited by Will DeRooy

Library of Congress Cataloging-in-Publication Data on file

Printed in the United States of America

17   16   15

10   9   8   7   6   5   4   3

Contents

✳ Part 1 ✳
Stepping Into Your Mindful Path: Core Mindfulness Skills

✱ Part 2 ✱
Applying Mindfulness: Handling Stressful Situations

✱ Part 3 ✱
Your Life Journey

Acknowledgments

I haven't invented anything new in *The Mindful Teen*. This book is a distillation of the experience and wisdom of leaders and teachers in the fields of mindfulness, mental health, and positive youth development. I have tried to share the fruits of my own personal mindfulness practice, as well as my clinical experience with teens as a pediatrician specializing in adolescent medicine. All trees have roots, and my root teacher in mindfulness for many years has been the Vietnamese Zen Master, poet, activist, and Nobel Peace Prize nominee Thich Nhat Hanh. Many of the mindfulness verses, guided meditations, practices, and concepts I share including sitting meditation, belly breathing, the body scan, informal mindfulness, mindful eating, walking meditation, loving-kindness meditation, mindful communication, and mindful peacemaking—have been inspired by Thich Nhat Hanh and by the practices of Plum Village, the meditation center that he founded in 1982 in the south of France.

That said, you certainly do not need to be Buddhist to benefit from mindfulness. Jon Kabat-Zinn, one of the pioneers of mindfulness in the West, is fond of saying that even the Buddha himself wasn't "Buddhist." In that spirit, I have done my best to present the practices in a secular, universal way—one that might appeal to diverse teens and families of any culture or religion (or no religion at all) and is appropriate for use in health care and educational settings.

In addition, *The Mindful Teen* is based on the MARS-A (Mindful Awareness and Resilience Skills for Adolescents) course that I developed with my friend and colleague Dr. Jake Locke and that is currently offered at the British Columbia Children's Hospital. MARS-A is a teen-friendly, developmentally appropriate, eight-week (nine-session) outpatient mindfulness-based intervention for adolescents (ages fifteen to nineteen) who are experiencing psychological distress (depressive symptoms, anxiety symptoms, or both), with or without co-occurring chronic pain or another chronic health condition. We modeled the basic structure and content of MARS-A on Mindfulness-Based Stress Reduction (MBSR) (Kabat-Zinn 2013), as well as on two subsequent adaptations of MBSR: Mindfulness-Based Cognitive Therapy (MBCT; Segal, Williams, and Teasdale 2013), and Mindfulness-Based Stress Reduction for Teens (MBSR-T; Biegel et al. 2009). Some of the core mindfulness practices in both MBSR and MBCT (including mindful eating, sitting meditation, mindful movement, walking meditation, the body scan, mindfulness of thinking, and informal mindfulness), as well as loving-kindness meditation (which comes from MBSR), are practiced in a modified form in MARS-A and presented in *The Mindful Teen* in a style that is heavily informed by both the teachings of Plum Village and my own personal mindfulness practice. The section on mindfulness of the body and handling pain (chapter 6) draws heavily from MBSR, and the sections on mindfulness of thinking (chapter 9) and self-care (chapter 17) draw heavily from MBCT.

MARS-A also draws heavily from the work on positive youth development by Kenneth Ginsburg—in particular, the sections on stress and coping (chapter 1) and perfectionism (chapter 11). MARS-A also draws from the work on interpersonal neurobiology by Daniel Siegel—in particular, the sections on the neurobiology of stress (chapter 1) and building connectedness (chapter 12).

I also owe a profound debt of gratitude to the many mentors, teachers, and colleagues who have supported me in this work, including but not limited to Kenneth Ginsburg, Colette (Coco) Auerswald, Jon Kabat-Zinn, Richard Kreipe, Ronald Epstein, Kim Schonert-Reichl, Adrianne Ross, Jeanie Seward-Magee, Thay Phap Hai, Sister Chan Khong, Curren Warf, Sabrina Gill, Amy Saltzman, Gina Biegel, Mark Bertin, Christopher Willard, Sheila Marshall, Andrea Johnson, Jane Garland, Deborah Christie, Margaret Callahan, Brian Callahan, Zindel Segal, Sarah Bowen, Steve Hickman, Catherine Phillips, Chris McKenna, Sam Himelstein, Larissa Duncan, Kevin Barrows, Mark Unno, Shimi Kang, and Nimi Singh. Thank you also to British Columbia Children's Hospital and to the Kelty Mental Health Resource Centre for supporting our mindfulness programs with teens. I thank those who have given so generously of their time and talents to review versions of the manuscript and make it better, including Mark Bertin, Jeanie Seward-Magee, Ly Hoang, Ly Nguyen, the publications team at Plum Village, and my editors—Tesilya Hanauer, Jess Beebe, and Will DeRooy.

To my loving partner in mindfulness and in life, Ly Hoang, thank you for your generous support and patience during the birthing of this book. To my mother, Ngoc Do, my deceased father, Han Vo (who was my first mindfulness teacher), and my sister, Ylan—thank you for your inspiration and guidance. I hope that my work in mindfulness can continue what you've shown me.

Most importantly, my heartfelt thanks to the teens who have shared their wisdom with me. May their wisdom and resilience inspire you, too.

Introduction

Dealing with Stress

My happiness grows in direct proportion to my acceptance
and in inverse proportion to my expectations.

— actor Michael J. Fox (2007)

Being a teenager can be really stressful. Maybe even at this
moment you are dealing with stress at school, in the form of
pressure to get better grades and to do more extracurricular
activities, filling up every moment of every day. Maybe you are
dealing with stress at home, in the form of financial problems,
arguments, or separations. Maybe your relationships with
your friends are stressful. Maybe dating or your involvement
in sports is stressful. Perhaps you are dealing with issues
having to do with bullying, discrimination, poverty, or
violence in your community. Maybe you are dealing with
chronic pain or some other chronic health condition, like
diabetes. On top of all that, you are probably trying to figure
out answers to big questions like *Who am I? Where do I fit in?
How can I become independent and make my own decisions?* It's no
wonder if you feel overwhelmed sometimes.

Any time you are experiencing a lot of stress, you may get "stuck" in your thoughts, whether you are worrying about the future or feeling bad about the past. You may get caught up in judgments about and emotional reactions to whatever is happening. If you don't know how to handle stress, you may do things that end up hurting yourself or the people around you. For this reason, learning how to handle stress effectively—in a healthy way—might just be the most important thing you can do to truly thrive, and reach your full potential.

Mindfulness is a simple but powerful tool for awakening the wisdom that is already inside of you. It can help you handle stressful situations and transform difficult relationships. With mindfulness, you can free yourself from those troublesome thoughts about the past or the future, becoming more present in the "here and now." Mindfulness also fosters the sort of kindness and compassion that can help you become your own best friend, as well as a better friend to others.

Resilience and Mindfulness

Resilience is your ability to thrive despite being faced with stressful situations. It's your power to rise above stress, to cope with challenges and bounce back. Imagine a suspension bridge, like the Golden Gate Bridge. In a storm, resilience is what allows the bridge to continue to stand strong, without collapsing. Resilience includes both outside supports and inner strengths. Outside supports are like the towers and cables holding up the bridge. Inner strengths are the things that are inside the bridge, helping it to be strong—its materials and construction.

Your own resilience helps you survive storms of stress and adversity. Your outside supports include things like having a caring adult in your life who really cares about you and is there for you, no matter what. That adult might be a parent, an aunt, a teacher, a coach, a counselor, or a doctor. Other really important outside supports are friends and peers who can help you make positive choices. Your inner strengths are your tools for coping with stress, such as your optimism, your perseverance, your creativity, and your coping skills.

Mindfulness can be another inner strength. Dr. Jon Kabat-Zinn, who has helped thousands of people at hospitals and clinics around the world learn and practice mindfulness as a way of dealing with pain and stress, defined mindfulness as "Paying attention in a particular way: on purpose, in the present moment, and nonjudgmentally" (1994, 4). It sounds simple, doesn't it? But it's not always easy. Infusing your life with mindfulness takes some training and practice. That's what this book is all about.

What I Do and Why I Wrote This Book

I'm a pediatrician specializing in adolescent medicine. Basically, that means I try to help teenagers be healthy, stay safe, and have a positive future. In my job at a children's hospital, I meet teens who experience intense stress. Some of them suffer health consequences like depression, anxiety, chronic pain, difficulty sleeping, and problems functioning at home and at school.

Fifteen years ago, I began learning the "art of mindful living" from the Vietnamese Zen Master, poet, activist, and Nobel Peace Prize nominee Thich Nhat Hanh. Since then, I've practiced mindfulness every day. It has really changed my life and helped me through some very stressful times.

Several years ago, I began to wonder, *If mindfulness has helped me so much, and it has helped so many other adults with stress, could it be useful for the teens I work with?* So I worked with my colleague Dr. Jake Locke to develop an eight-week mindfulness course for teens at our hospital. The course is called Mindful Awareness and Resilience Skills for Adolescents (MARS-A). Most of what you will learn in this book comes from my own experience and the experiences of teens taking MARS-A.

I am delighted to be sharing mindfulness with you. Some adults have said that teens can't learn mindfulness: that teens are either too immature or don't have the patience and attention span to be truly mindful. My experience has been the exact opposite. The teens I have worked with have proven to me that they really "get it," even more than many adults. I've witnessed some amazing and inspiring transformation and healing among these teens. They have told me that mindfulness practice helps them do the following:

* Handle everyday stress

* Handle anxiety before taking a test at school

* Enjoy daily activities like taking the bus or walking the dog

* Handle arguments with parents and friends

* Concentrate in class

* Handle repetitive negative thoughts, like memories, worries, and regrets

* Improve their relationships with friends and significant others

* Handle difficult moods, like depression and anxiety

* Stay in school instead of needing to go home when they are feeling bad

Is Mindfulness a Religion?

Mindfulness meditation has been practiced for thousands of years in Buddhist cultures, and many of the practices in this book are inspired by Buddhist meditation. But mindfulness is also found in other wisdom traditions throughout the world, even if it's not always called "mindfulness." For example, the thirteenth-century Persian poet Jalal ad-Din ar-Rumi, the nineteenth-century American transcendentalist poet Henry David Thoreau, and the twentieth-century Catholic nun and Nobel Peace Prize winner Mother Teresa all wrote movingly about the practice of dwelling deeply in the present moment, with a fully open heart. Mindfulness can be beneficial for everybody, no matter who you are or where you come from. In other words, you don't need to be a Buddhist to meditate. You can be any religion, or you can be no religion at all. Mindfulness doesn't ask you to believe anything, and it doesn't ask you *not* to believe anything. It's all about paying attention, cultivating your compassion, and learning from your own observations and experience.

How to Use This Book

The best way to read this book is with an open mind and an open heart. For now, try to let go of any expectations or ideas you have about mindfulness. This includes negative expectations, like *This whole meditation thing is stupid and would never work for me*. It also includes any positive expectations, like *Mindfulness is going to solve all my problems*. Instead, approach the practice of mindfulness in the spirit of playful experimentation—*I'm going to try this out and see whether anything interesting happens*.

Part 1 of this book (chapters 1 to 9) is like a how-to manual that will teach you core mindfulness practices. Some examples are mindful breathing, sitting meditation, the body scan, and practices for handling difficult thoughts, feelings, and emotions with mindfulness. You'll also learn "informal mindfulness," which involves bringing that same mindful awareness into your everyday activities, like eating lunch and walking to school. You'll see the words "mindfulness" and "meditation" used interchangeably. For the purposes of this book, you can consider those two words to mean the same thing.

In part 2 (chapters 10 to 16), we will explore how to use mindfulness practices to handle stress in specific situations. For example, you'll learn how to use mindfulness to handle stress at school, at home, and when you are experiencing conflict with your peers or classmates. In part 3 (chapters 17 and 18), we will explore how to sustain a mindfulness practice, which will help you make your life path a mindful journey.

In the "Try This!" sections, I'll walk you through specific mindfulness practices. Some of these you can practice with the help of audio recordings available at http://www .newharbinger.com/30802. These recordings, called *guided meditations,* will allow you to close your eyes while you follow the instructions or narration. I hope that you try each practice at least once, in the spirit of open-minded experimentation, just to see what you notice. If you find a particular practice beneficial, maybe it can become part of your everyday life.

I have been teaching mindfulness to teens for over four years now at the children's hospital where I work. The ways in which teens have said that their mindfulness practice has touched their lives continue to inspire me. In this book are stories (like "Lisa's Story" in chapter 1) about how some of those teens learned to practice mindfulness, featuring things they shared in class. In the "Teen Voices" sections are other things that teens have said about mindfulness. I hope that their words and mine inspire you to discover your own powers of mindfulness and resilience, which will support you on the sometimes difficult journey to adulthood and beyond.

Teen Voices: *Nicole R.*

"Before learning about mindfulness and practicing it, I had not realized how much of my life I was living outside of the present moment. I am a very anxious person, and I'm often worrying about the future or the past. Mindfulness has allowed me to live more in the now. I feel a sense of self-awareness that I didn't have before, and it has been incredibly useful for managing my anxiety.

"As youth we get so caught up in trying to do as much as we can, as well as we can, to please as many people as we can, that we don't take time to enjoy anything. We don't take enough time to love ourselves or really listen to ourselves. Mindfulness helps you do that.

"One of the best things about mindfulness is that…[t]here are so many ways to live a more mindful life. Mindfulness is beyond just sitting meditations or yoga practices.

"I think that mindfulness can benefit everyone. In the beginning, you may feel silly or find it hard, but it will get easier. You just have to approach it with an open mind and no expectations. Don't be afraid to have fun with your mindfulness practice or to be creative. Don't be afraid to tell people about it or encourage others to do it with you.

"The hardest part is getting yourself to do it. The next hardest part is getting yourself to stick with it. Everything else is much easier."

✳ Part 1 ✳

Stepping into Your Mindful Path: Core Mindfulness Skills

Chapter 1

Stress, Health, and Coping

The longer I live the more convinced I become that life is 10 percent what happens to us and 90 percent how we react to it.

— pastor and educator
Charles R. Swindoll (2009)

If you had to, how would you define "stress"? Here are some examples:

"Feeling really worried about something."

"Being overwhelmed by stuff."

"When there's too much going on and I can't deal with it."

"Feeling so frustrated that I want to scream."

Stress arises in response to a challenging situation in your life, and it can be really difficult to handle. But knowledge is power: once you understand what stress does to your body and your mind, you will be empowered to handle it more effectively.

✱ Lisa's Story

Lisa had had almost constant pain in her back since a car accident about two years earlier. The pain, she said, had caused major stress in her life; because of the stress, she was falling behind in school and getting into lots of arguments with her dad at home. She was also feeling really tired all the time.

In our first meeting, Lisa said, "I wish I hadn't gotten in that accident. If it wasn't for that accident, everything would be fine." She said she worried a lot about her future, her college applications (she was a senior in high school), and her grades. "What if my pain never gets better? What if I can't finish high school? What if I can't go to college?"

Lisa soon learned to recognize—by paying attention to her own thoughts—that her regrets about the past and her worries about the future were making her stress and pain worse. She discovered that she could use meditation practices such as mindful breathing (which you'll learn in chapter 2) and the body scan (which you'll learn in chapter 6) to bring herself back to the present moment.

After eight weeks of meditating, Lisa said she had noticed that her energy level had increased. "I never realized how tiring it was to be so stressed out all the time!" she remarked. She had also started to let go of her stress about the future. "Instead of worrying about college and university, I can just focus on what I have to do right now."

What Is Stress? The "Fight, Flight, or Freeze" Response

Your body and your mind are amazing. Believe it or not, it's actually a good thing that you are able to experience stress! I know that sounds a little weird. Stress feels really uncomfortable—so how could it possibly be a good thing?

Your body's stress response is designed to help you survive danger. And it's really good at helping you survive the kinds of dangers—like being attacked by a tiger—that threatened your ancestors' survival thousands of years ago. The stress response is also called the "fight, flight, or freeze" response, which tells you a lot about how it works. If you were being attacked by a tiger, your stress response would help you fight back more strongly ("fight"), run away more quickly ("flight"), or hide more quietly or play dead more convincingly ("freeze"). Let's look at how the stress response affects your body and your mind.

The Stress Response in Your Body

Let's say you're in the wilderness somewhere, when suddenly a tiger appears close by. As soon as you see the tiger, your brain sends signals to different parts of your body through nerve impulses, as well as through hormones such as adrenaline. These signals have immediate and powerful effects throughout your entire body.

13

* **Your heart.** Your heart starts racing—beating faster and pumping blood harder. This provides more blood to the muscles in your body, which will help you fight back with more strength or run away more quickly.

* **Your lungs.** Your breath gets quicker and shallower, to supply more oxygen to your heart and other muscles.

* **Your muscles.** Your leg muscles get tense, ready to run away. Your arm muscles get tense, ready to fight. The muscles around your neck, shoulders, and face also tense up, to help you be more alert.

* **Your stomach and intestines.** In fight, flight, or freeze mode, most of your blood is directed to your heart, lungs, and muscles. At the same time, your intestines squeeze and empty, as blood rushes away from them. Different people experience this in different ways. Maybe you've heard expressions like "I was so scared I pooped my pants," "That made me want to throw up," or "I got butterflies in my stomach."

Everyone experiences the fight, flight, or freeze response a little differently. How about you? Have you ever noticed the stress response happening in your own body when you've been stressed, scared, or anxious? In these moments, have you felt your own heart racing, felt your breathing speed up, felt your muscles get tense, or felt a sick feeling in your stomach?

Stress and the Brain

Your body and your brain are deeply connected; they constantly send signals back and forth. What happens in your body has huge effects on your brain, and what happens in your brain has powerful effects on your body. The "hand model of the brain" (Siegel 2010) is a good way to understand what's happening in your brain when your stress response—your fight, flight, or freeze response—is activated.

Exercise: Hand Model of the Brain

While sitting or standing, bend your left elbow so that your palm points up toward the ceiling. Look at your arm and imagine that it represents your whole body. Your wrist is your neck, and your hand is your brain.

Now, curl your thumb into your palm. Your thumb and your palm represent the deepest-lying parts of your brain. Doctors and scientists call these parts the subcortical or limbic areas. For the purposes of this book, let's call this area the "lizard brain," because the brains of lizards look almost exactly the same as this primitive part of our brains. The lizard brain is your brain's "alarm system"—its main job is to warn you of danger.

Now, curl your other four fingers down, over your thumb. See the front parts of your middle two fingers? We can call that your "human brain." Doctors and scientists call it the prefrontal cortex. Your human brain is responsible for all the qualities that make you truly human. This part of your brain helps you do the following:

- See a situation clearly.

- Think rationally.

- Make smart decisions.

- Act with wisdom and compassion.

Now, let's look at what happens when your stress response gets activated. Whenever your brain perceives a threat, your body switches into fight, flight, or freeze mode and activates your lizard brain. Your lizard brain makes you experience intense emotions, like stress or fear or anger. The problem is the lizard brain isn't very smart—its only concern is to deal with threats to your immediate safety. Therefore, when your lizard brain is activated, it often seems as though everything and everyone is attacking you, even if they're not. Your perception is distorted because you're seeing the world through a lens of intense emotion.

Sometimes, your lizard brain can overwhelm your human brain—especially when you are tired, when you are feeling hungry, or when you haven't had enough sleep. Let's look again at the hand model of the brain. Your human brain is represented by your fingers curled over your thumb. Now, flip your fingers back upward to imagine what happens when you get stressed: Your lizard brain gets activated and overwhelms your human brain, and you "flip your lid" or "lose your mind." Before you know it, maybe you've said something or done something to hurt yourself or someone else. Maybe you've yelled, screamed, broke something, or hit someone.

Has that ever happened to you?

I know that it has happened to me—many times, in fact. Flipping out or losing your mind under stressful conditions is a very human thing to do. As a teen, you are more prone to flip your lid and lose your mind than most adults, because the "human" part of your brain is still growing and developing rapidly (and it will continue to develop significantly until you're well into your twenties). But your lizard brain is already quite well developed.

Here's another question: How long does it take for your lizard brain to be activated and for you to flip your lid? In my experience, it can happen in less than one second!

Here's the good news: even when you lose your mind, your human brain hasn't gone anywhere. It's always there for you. As soon as you recognize, *Whoa, my lizard brain is getting activated right now!* you have an opportunity to step back, take a break, and reconnect with your human brain. And with your human brain back online, you'll be able to see the situation more clearly and respond in a way that's healthier for you and healthier for the people around you.

"Paper Tigers"

If you were really being attacked by a tiger, your stress response would help you survive. Probably, though, most of the stress in your life comes from things like school, your relationships, your parents, and conflict with other teens or adults.

The problem is sometimes your body and mind can't tell the difference between real danger—actual threats to your life, like tigers—and other types of dangers you perceive. An exam at school or an argument with your mom can activate your stress response just as if you were being attacked by a tiger. In other words, whether you are facing a real tiger or a "paper tiger," your brain and body react in almost exactly the same way. Even worried and negative thinking—tigers in your mind—can trigger your fight, flight, or freeze response!

Acute vs. Chronic Stress

A little bit of stress can be good for you—it can help you be more alert, focus, have more energy, and perform better. The problem is when your stress level gets too high or stays high for too long. Chronic stress can lead to serious mental health problems, such as depression, in which your mood and energy get so low that your life is dragged down; or it can lead to anxiety, filling your days with worries, nervousness, and panic. Because of the way the brain and body are connected, chronic stress also affects almost every organ in your body. It can lead to headaches, digestive problems, muscle pain, fatigue, difficulty sleeping, and many other health problems. So, it's crucial for your health that you learn effective ways of handling stress.

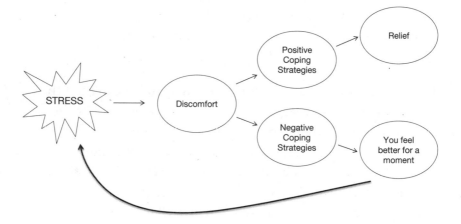

Figure 1: Positive and Negative Coping
Adapted with permission from Kenneth Ginsburg.

Positive and Negative Coping

Stress makes you feel very uncomfortable. Whenever you are feeling stressed, you naturally want to do something to try to help yourself feel better. There are generally two different ways that you can respond to stress: positive and negative coping.

Negative coping behaviors are attempts to escape or cover up stress in ways that might be harmful to yourself or to someone else. Can you think of some examples of negative coping behaviors in teens? How about smoking, getting drunk or getting high, fighting or yelling, running away, skipping school, engaging in self-harm (like cutting yourself), video game and Internet addiction, or starving yourself (anorexia) or making yourself throw up (bulimia)?

I'm not here to judge you or anyone else. I'm also not calling these behaviors "negative" because they don't work. In fact, sometimes these strategies do work. If you're stressed out and you try one of these negative coping behaviors, you might start to feel better very quickly, at least for a moment. The problem is, in the long term, there's a good chance that you'll end up creating an even more stressful situation. For example, you might get into trouble, damage a friendship or relationship, get kicked out of school, or even end up in the hospital. Negative coping leads to more stress, and it harms you and the people around you.

On the other hand, positive coping also helps you handle stress, but in ways that are more healthy. Can you think of some examples of positive coping that you use or know about?

19

How about going for a walk, talking to a trusted friend or adult, listening to relaxing music, exercising, or having a healthy snack? Practicing mindfulness is also an example of positive coping.

Usually when you choose negative coping, it is a sign that your lizard brain is activated. If you can access the clear thinking and wisdom of your human brain when you are stressed, you will be more likely to choose a positive coping strategy. Another difference between positive and negative coping is that positive coping strategies may not help you right away. They may take some time and practice. But it's worth it. After you learn and use positive coping strategies, you'll feel better for longer, and you won't end up causing yourself more stress.

Try This! Be Mindful of Your Stress Response

Next time you are worried, stressed out, or overwhelmed, take a few minutes just to tune in to your body and your mind, to see what your own stress response is like. Tune in to your heartbeat. Do you feel your heartbeat getting faster, your heart pounding in your chest? Tune in to your breath: is it getting faster, shallower? Check in with the muscles in your arms, back, and neck: are they getting tight and tense? What about your stomach—is it feeling sore or sick?

At the same time, take a moment to check in with your thoughts and feelings. Are negative thoughts, worries, and fear flooding your mind? Is your lizard brain activated?

Just being aware of your stress response creates a moment of awareness, a moment of mindfulness. You can say silently to yourself, *I know that my lizard brain is activated right now; I'm going to take a break and go chill somewhere else for a few minutes.* Take some long, deep breaths, and see whether this allows your human brain to come back online.

The following quotes are from teens describing how mindfulness practice had helped them in general.

---Teen Voices---

"I've got a tool now to deal with my pain, anxiety, and stress."
—Grace

"If I practiced mindfulness every day, I would be a very calm and happy person." —Bailey

"It helps me get relaxed before my day really starts; walking to school, it helps me feel less anxious about school." —Mitesh

You don't have to let stress make you into a victim. What you do and how you think can transform the stress response in your body and your mind. You have a lot of power and strength to manage your stress response in a healthy way, in a way that is better for you and for the people around you. Mindfulness practice is a powerful way of reengaging your human brain and handling stress with more wisdom. That's what we'll explore together for the rest of the book.

Chapter 2

Wake Up Now!
Autopilot vs. Awareness

> Be happy in the moment—that's enough.
> Each moment is all we need, not more.
>
> — Mother Teresa

Stress will arise in your life, whether you want it to or not—
but how you relate to it is totally up to you. Mindfulness
can give you a powerful tool for increasing your resiliency
and helping you rise above difficulty. You already know that
life as a teen is stressful. The truth is that life as an adult
is also stressful. Learning how to handle stress now, while
you're young, can help you have a positive future as an adult.
Mindfulness is something you can practice and use now and
for the rest of your life. So why wait?

Shift out of Autopilot

Have you ever been so preoccupied that you weren't consciously aware of what you were actually doing? For example, have you ever walked from one class to another, and found that by the time you arrived you didn't even remember how you got there? Maybe you were busy checking your phone, or rushing just to get there on time, or thinking about what you needed to do later. And suddenly you "woke up" and realized where you were.

Perhaps you go through much of your life as if in a dream, mindlessly, without awareness. Your body may be in one place, and your mind may be somewhere else. We call this being "on autopilot," as if you are cruising through life automatically, robotically. We all have a strong tendency to let our autopilot take over as we go through our daily lives.

✳ *Mary's Story*

Mary said that she had been getting stressed out a lot by drama with her friends and drama with her family. Her stress was sometimes so severe that she got headaches and belly pain. She sometimes missed school because of it. She didn't know what she could do to handle her stress, and she felt hopeless.

At the start of the mindfulness course, Mary was skeptical. The main reason she had agreed to take the course was because her mother had pressured her to. But she decided, as she said, "I'm here now—I might as well give it a try. I'm already really stressed out—what do I have to lose?" So she tried some short formal mindfulness practices at home, like mindful breathing (which you'll learn in this chapter), sitting meditation (which you'll learn in chapter 4), and the body scan (which you'll learn in chapter 6). She also started to practice mindfulness informally—bringing that same present-moment, nonjudgmental awareness to activities like walking, sitting on the bus, and brushing her teeth.

By paying attention to her own life and her own stress, Mary said she was surprised to learn that she spent a lot of time on autopilot and that being on autopilot usually worsened her stress. At the end of the mindfulness course, Mary said, "Now I know how to handle stress and pain in a healthy way, and I do feel that it has helped me a lot…in many different situations."

Any time you are going through life on autopilot, you might take for granted all kinds of seemingly "ordinary" experiences. If you can shift out of autopilot and into a deep present-moment awareness, you can discover how *extraordinary* every moment of life can be. If you can be fully present, you can experience the miracle of being truly alive even while doing the simplest of activities, such as eating a raisin.

Try This! Eat a Raisin Mindfully

You can do this mindfulness practice using the instructions below or with the help of the recording (track 1) available at http://www.newharbinger .com/30802.

Start by placing a single raisin on a table or plate in front of you. (If you are allergic to raisins, or if you don't have any raisins handy, you can substitute some other food that is easily available and that you have eaten before, like an orange, some peanuts, or even a piece of candy.)

Perhaps you have certain ideas about what a raisin is, what a raisin looks like, or what a raisin tastes like. Perhaps you like raisins, or perhaps you don't. For now, put all your ideas and expectations about raisins aside. For now, simply experience and explore this raisin as if you had never encountered a raisin before. Imagine that you're an alien and you've just arrived on Earth. You are very curious to explore new things about Earth, and today is your chance to find out what a raisin is all about. You are going to explore this raisin with all of your senses. You are going to be really curious about this particular, individual raisin in great detail and try to get to know it.

Before you do anything with the raisin, start by coming fully to the present moment. Tell yourself you have nothing else to do and nowhere to go right now. Take three breaths in and out. As best you can, just bring your full attention to the here and now.

Begin to inspect the raisin with your sense of sight. Hold the raisin up in your hand. Take a good, slow, long look at it. What do you notice about what this raisin looks like? What do you notice about its color? Its texture? Does it look different depending on the angle or the light? Take your time looking at the raisin; there's no need to rush.

Now, examine the raisin with your sense of touch. Roll it between your thumb and your index finger, squeeze it gently, or rub it slowly. What do you notice? How does the raisin feel? Is it warm or cool? Firm or soft? Again, take your time examining the raisin in detail, with great curiosity.

If all this seems a bit silly, that's okay. This is just an experiment. You can approach it with a sense of playfulness. Even though your mom may have told you when you were little not to play with your food, for now it's okay.

Now, examine the raisin with your sense of smell. Hold it up to your nose, close your eyes, and gently breathe in through your nostrils. What do you notice? Do you smell anything? Is it a faint smell, or a strong smell? Is it sweet, or is it bitter?

Next, examine the raisin with your sense of hearing. Hold the raisin up to one ear. Give it a gentle squeeze, or roll it between your thumb and your index finger. Do you hear anything? Remember, this is the first time you have touched a raisin, so you don't know what to expect. Just be curious, and be open to whatever you experience, letting go of any expectations.

After listening to the raisin for a minute or two, place the raisin in your mouth, on the middle of your tongue. If you notice the urge to chew or swallow, try to just notice that urge, without acting on it right away. As the raisin sits on your tongue, roll it around your mouth, from front to back and side to side. What do you notice about the texture of the raisin as you roll it around in your mouth? Do you notice your mouth or body responding in any way to the presence of this raisin in your mouth? You can put the book down and close your eyes for a minute or two while you do this.

Now, gently bite down on the raisin. Chew it very slowly, with purpose and care, paying close attention to every detail of taste, sensation, and texture as you chew. Take your time, slowly chewing the raisin until it dissolves. What does it taste like? What is happening to the texture, the consistency, of the raisin? You can put the book down for this part too and close your eyes as you chew the raisin.

If a thought like *I don't like raisins* or *This doesn't taste good* enters your mind, just notice you are having a judgmental thought. Then, as best you can, bring your attention back to the pure sensory experience of the raisin in your mouth.

When the raisin is almost completely dissolved, go ahead and slowly—intentionally—swallow it. Notice what it feels like as the raisin goes down your throat, toward your stomach.

After the raisin is gone, pause and take a moment to thank yourself for eating a raisin mindfully. Thanking yourself is a way to practice self-compassion, which (as you'll learn in chapter 3) is an essential ingredient in mindfulness practice.

Here are a few questions to reflect on after eating a raisin mindfully:

1. What did you notice while eating the raisin and paying very close attention? I don't mean what did you *think* about the raisin. I mean, what did you *experience directly*, with your senses of sight, hearing, touch, smell, and taste?

2. How is what you just did any different from the way you would normally eat a raisin?

3. What could eating a raisin slowly and carefully possibly have to do with managing stress?

Personally, I have a tendency to eat raisins quickly—usually in my cereal—without thinking about it. When I eat a raisin slowly and mindfully, I notice many things that I don't normally notice. I notice that different parts of the raisin might be different colors. I'm surprised by the little squeaky noise when I squeeze it next to my ear. I notice how much taste and flavor a single raisin has. I am surprised at how enjoyable eating a raisin can be, even though usually I think that I don't "like" raisins (and haven't, ever since I was a little kid!).

Perhaps you've eaten thousands of raisins. You might normally eat raisins on autopilot—just going through the motions, while your mind is somewhere else. When you take time to slow down and intentionally pay attention to something so simple, your experience can become richer, fuller, more alive—more flavorful. Perhaps even more delicious!

You can shift out of autopilot and into present-moment awareness while eating a raisin, while sitting quietly and focusing on your breath, or while doing almost any other activity. When you pay attention with curiosity and openhearted awareness, you will begin to free yourself from your own judgments and expectations. You will experience life *just as it is*, moment to moment. This can be profoundly liberating, helping you free yourself from stress.

The Many Definitions of Mindfulness

Asking someone to define mindfulness is kind of like asking, "What does chocolate taste like?" Or "What does your favorite song sound like?" Definitions can only give you a small idea of the real experience. Just reading about mindfulness without experiencing it yourself is like going to a restaurant to read the menu, without tasting any of the food. Just as the point of going to a restaurant is to taste the food, the point of mindfulness is to actually experience it.

That said, there are some descriptions of mindfulness that might be a good place to start. Jon Kabat-Zinn's definition of mindfulness as "paying attention in a particular way: on purpose, in the present moment, and nonjudgmentally" (1994, 4) is simple and to the point. Mindfulness is all about paying attention to the present moment. Mindfulness is about shifting out of autopilot and awakening to the here and now. Mindfulness is about freeing yourself from regrets about the past and worries about the future.

Here are a few other ways of describing mindfulness:

* "Being present"

* "Awareness"

* "Awakening"

* "Concentration plus attention"

* "Seeing clearly"

* "Compassionate awareness"

* "Openheartedness"

* "Loving presence"

People in every culture around the world have recognized the wisdom of openhearted, present-moment awareness, whether or not they called it "mindfulness," for thousands of years. Everyone can be mindful. You have probably already experienced moments of natural mindfulness. Perhaps you've had times, without even trying to, when you were deeply aware of what you were doing; the only thing that mattered was the present moment—the past and the future seemed to disappear—and you were filled with gratitude for being alive. Maybe this happens for you when you play sports. Or maybe you experience this kind of awareness when you play a musical instrument, when you pet your dog or cat gently, or when you listen to your favorite song. Whether you realized it or not in those moments, you already know how to be mindful!

Breathing: The Heart of Mindfulness

You breathe in and out about twenty thousand times a day. How many of those breaths are you consciously aware of? How many of those breaths do you really enjoy? If you're like most people, the answer is "not many." The foundation of all mindfulness practices is to bring your awareness to your breath. This is also known as "coming back to your breath." Your breath is a wonderful gift that brings your mind and body together in the here and now. You can start to bring yourself back to the present moment, and begin to free yourself from stress, with as few as three mindful breaths. Right here. Right now. Give it a try.

Try This! Mindful Breathing

You can do this mindfulness practice using the instructions below or with the help of the recording (track 2) available at http://www.newharbinger .com/30802. *I recommend that you start by following along with the recording a few times. Then, try guiding yourself through the practice, without the recording, just to see what that's like.*

First, stop. Stop whatever you are doing, or whatever it is that you were about to do, and simply allow yourself to be "here," without needing to do anything.

Next, simply bring your attention to your breath, just as it is, in the here and now. You don't need to make your breath any different than it naturally is. You don't have to make it slower or deeper. Just bring your attention to your natural breath, with an attitude of curiosity and kindness. Notice the movement of the air as you breathe in, inhaling oxygen, and as you breathe out, exhaling carbon dioxide.

Experiment with saying silently to yourself as you breathe in and out, *Breathing in, I know that I am breathing in. Breathing out, I know that I am breathing out* (Nhat Hanh 2009, 4). Or, you can shorten this to *In. Out.*

Pay careful attention to your breath, following it as you breathe in and out. Notice the beginning of your in-breath. Follow your in-breath from the beginning, to the middle, all the way to the end. Then notice the pause between your in-breath and your out-breath. Follow your out-breath from the beginning, to the middle, all the way to the end.

You might want to imagine that you are floating in the ocean and each breath is a wave passing beneath you. Each in-breath lifts you up, and each out-breath sets you back down. Just float gently on the waves of your breath. It might also help to focus on the part of your body where you notice your breath most easily, like your nose—where you can feel the air going in and out—or your belly, which expands and contracts with each breath.

Following your breath doesn't have to feel like work. Breathing mindfully can be relaxing and enjoyable. If your breath feels good, simply enjoy the sensation and smile.

If your mind wanders or if you get distracted, that's okay. That's what minds do. Don't judge yourself as having done something "wrong." You can just notice and gently say to yourself, *Oh, my mind has wandered off*, and perhaps be curious about where your mind wandered off to. Then gently bring your attention back to the next breath.

You can breathe mindfully like this for three breaths, nine breaths, or, if you have time, two or three minutes.

What was it like to pay attention to your breath? What was it like to come back to the present moment? Did you notice anything interesting or surprising?

You can take some time to do mindful breathing any time of day, anywhere. After breathing mindfully for a few breaths or a few minutes, continue to go about your day, more connected to the present moment. See whether coming back to your breath changes your day in any way. Your breath is always there for you, to keep you alive and nourish your body and your mind. Can you learn to be there for your breath?

Chapter 3

Opening Your Heart and Mind to Free Yourself from Stress

In Asian languages, the word for "mind" and the word for "heart" are [the same]. So if you're not hearing mindfulness in some deep way as heartfulness, you're not really understanding it. Compassion and kindness towards oneself are intrinsically woven into it. You could think of mindfulness as wise and affectionate attention.

— Jon Kabat-Zinn (2012)

In the past, perhaps you have tried to run away from stress. Trying to deal with stress by running away from it works only up to a point and often makes things worse in the end. Yet paying attention to your stress can feel even *more* stressful, if you don't know how to handle your stress wisely. That's where "the mindful spirit" comes in. Mindfulness isn't just about paying attention—it's about paying attention *in a different way*.

With the mindful spirit, mindfulness takes on the power to heal and transform stress.

In this chapter, we will explore three essential qualities or attitudes that make up the mindful spirit: beginner's mind, loving-kindness, and self-compassion. Beginner's mind will help you see situations with an open mind, bring a childlike joy to every moment, and let go of judgments that can increase your stress. Loving-kindness and self-compassion will allow you to hold your stress and difficulty with an open heart.

By tapping into the healing powers of your heart as well as your mind, you can learn to simply breathe while being aware of your stress, instead of running away from it. Only once you can stay with your stress in this way and "hold it gently"—inviting your mindful spirit to help you stay present and take care of your stress—will you have a chance to heal it and to free yourself from it.

Beginner's Mind

When you're a beginner, there's no pressure. There's no expectation of you to be an "expert," to have any answers, or to know anything. For example, kindergarteners are not expected to know how to read, which allows them to explore the world of books with joy and curiosity. Being a beginner is incredibly freeing. It allows you to be curious and to know the joy of discovery.

✱ Jason's Story

One day in class, we were about to have pizza. Before we started eating, I said, "Let's eat this pizza with beginner's mind. Let's eat the pizza as if we've never eaten pizza before— as if it is a new experience, an opportunity to try something really different and interesting. Take your time, and see what you notice that you might not normally notice."

After we ate, I asked the participants to share about the experience. Jason said, "I really love pizza. So I was tempted to just eat the pizza like I normally do, which means as fast as I can! But then I remembered what we talked about, slowing down and savoring it. So, I tried that. I was really surprised by it. I realized how many parts to the pizza there were. It wasn't just a piece of pizza. It was the crust, the cheese, the bell peppers, the mushrooms… I used to think that eating a piece of pizza was just all one thing, all lumped together. There was so much more to it than I had ever realized before. And, it tastes so much better eating it this way!"

Jason learned how interesting the simple act of eating pizza can be. He had eaten pizza many times before, so he had assumed that he already knew what pizza was all about. But when he ate pizza with beginner's mind, he discovered some interesting, surprising things that he hadn't noticed before.

Perhaps you had a similar experience when you tried the "Eat a Raisin" exercise in chapter 2. Eating a raisin mindfully is also a practice of beginner's mind: You let go of your ideas about what a raisin is like, and you simply experience eating that raisin wholeheartedly, using all your senses, with a childlike sense of wonder and curiosity. With beginner's mind, you experience each moment and each experience as if for the very first time. Whether you are doing something you do every day (like eating a piece of pizza or walking to the bus stop) or something really "special" (like meeting a newborn baby), that spirit of curiosity and openness can help every moment and every experience come alive.

Try This! Beginner's Mind and Your Own Inner Child

You can learn a lot about mindfulness by closely observing young children. Take a moment to remember the last time you took a walk with a young child (for example, three or four years old). Maybe you were walking on the beach or through the forest. Or maybe you were walking down the sidewalk in your neighborhood, to the park. Or perhaps you might remember what walking to the park or playing in a sandbox was like for you as a child.

What do you think that experience was like for that young child? What was it like for him or her just to walk and look around and explore the world?

Did the child become fascinated by something as ordinary as a leaf, a tree, or a rock? Was the child delighted and entertained by the common sight of a bug on the ground or a cloud floating by?

When you were a young child, you naturally approached every experience with the same beginner's mind. That's because every experience—learning to walk, learning to talk, meeting new people—actually was new to you at that time.

I invite you to get back in touch with your own beginner's mind. Bring your beginner's mind to an activity that seems routine or boring, like eating pizza or walking to the bus stop. Reawaken your inner child, and experience the joy, awe, and wonder of seeing the world as though everything were new.

Loving-Kindness

Loving-kindness can also be called heartfulness, compassion, friendliness, goodwill, or respect. Practicing mindfulness with the spirit of loving-kindness involves becoming fully present with whatever is happening inside you and around you, and meeting it with kindness.

✱ Bonnie's Story

Bonnie shared that she had recently begun hanging out with an old friend whom she had stopped hanging out with a while back. One day, she said, she started getting really annoyed with this friend and remembered why she had stopped hanging out with her. Only this time, she decided to practice a loving-kindness meditation (which you'll learn in chapter 12). As she said, "I remember reading a quote about how forgiving someone else is really a gift to yourself. It's not about whether the person deserves it or not. So I decided to try forgiving her, and I practiced the loving-kindness meditation. I tried to let it be, to let it go."

"So what happened?" I asked Bonnie.

"It made me feel a lot less tired. Less full of thoughts and judgments. Less stressed about the whole situation… It helped me remember the things about her that I actually do like, and we ended up having a nice day together."

Mindfulness is sometimes described as a bird with two wings: awareness and compassion. The practice needs both wings to take flight. Whenever stress and difficulty arise, awareness will allow you to understand what is happening and why. For example, Bonnie recognized, *I'm stressed right now because my friend is being really annoying.* Compassion will allow you to relate to your situation with kindness. Bonnie practiced compassion for her friend, saying silently to herself, *I'm going be nice to my friend anyway and see whether that helps make our afternoon together more fun.*

One of the best ways to cultivate loving-kindness is by intentionally smiling. You can smile to anyone and anything, whether pleasant or difficult. You can smile to your breath; you can smile to your neighbor; you can even smile to the exam at school that is stressing you out. Sending friendliness in this way, you can begin to let go of your stress. And, happiness is contagious—so help spread it around!

You already have loving-kindness inside of you. Through mindfulness, you can awaken it and intentionally bring it to bear in more situations in your life—stressful as well as pleasant ones.

Exercise: Get in Touch with Your Innate Loving-Kindness

Take a moment to imagine a small puppy or kitten. You might even want to remember your own cat or dog when he or she was very young. Imagine how beautiful, and also how vulnerable, that puppy or kitten is. Imagine holding it.

As you picture that cuddly creature in your arms, you may notice nurturing feelings arising inside you. You want to protect that animal; you want it to be well, and happy, and safe. What you are experiencing in this moment is loving-kindness. You may notice perhaps a warm sensation in your body, a certain feeling or emotion, or a beautiful thought, wish, or hope. What do you notice as you touch your innate loving-kindness?

Self-Compassion

Some of the teens I work with have a very hard time being kind toward themselves. Is that true for you? Do you sometimes hear a negative and self-critical inner voice saying things like the following?

* *I'm not good enough.*

* *I'm not smart enough.*

* *Everyone's judging me.*

* *It's all my fault.*

If these kinds of self-judgmental thoughts are familiar to you, that's okay. We all have them sometimes. But believing these self-judgments as if they were true can cause an enormous amount of stress.

Self-compassion means being fully present and friendly with everything inside of yourself, including all your thoughts, emotions, and feelings. It means accepting yourself completely, with compassion, just as you are. Mindfulness is a deeply nonviolent practice—there is no need to fight, reject, or deny your own stress or difficulties. A meditation teacher once said, "We don't have to 'let go' of our suffering, our difficult thoughts, emotions, or feelings. When we meet them with kindness, they let go of us." Meeting your stress with acceptance and self-compassion will allow you to soothe and calm your lizard brain, reducing your stress.

✳ *Eric's Story*

Eric had arthritis, which caused chronic pain in his hands, wrists, elbows, and knees. He had missed three months of school the previous year due to pain, stress, and anxiety. Observing his sensations and emotions mindfully helped him discover how connected all of those things were: "I missed school because I had joint pain. Then I got stressed and anxious about what I had missed. That just made my joint pain worse. So I had to miss more school. It became a cycle."

Eric shared that mindfulness meditation practices like mindful breathing and the body scan (which you'll learn in chapter 6) helped him get out of that destructive cycle. "With mindfulness, I found a way that I could lessen my anxiety, which lessened my joint pain. Then, I was able to start going back to school." He also practiced being kind and gentle with himself as he adjusted to getting back to school. "I used to be really hard on myself about grades," he explained. "Before, I would be really upset at myself if I got anything less than an A. But now, I just practice accepting myself. I'm even proud of myself just for being back in school and going every day. I can accept myself if I get a B or a C. I don't get so anxious about it anymore, and my pain doesn't get worse because of that."

When you're feeling stressed, you may have a hard time believing that you deserve compassion. But you deserve to be loved just as much as anyone. In fact, you have to learn how to love yourself unconditionally before you can be a true friend to anyone else. A true friend knows everything about you—your strengths and your weaknesses—and sticks by you anyway, no matter what. Can you become your own best friend?

Try This! Handle Stress with Your Innate Mindful Qualities

In moments of stress, get in touch with your beginner's mind, loving-kindness, and self-compassion. First, simply recognize right away that stress is arising. That moment of recognition is a real awakening—a precious opportunity to stop, reengage your human brain, and respond wisely.

Next, become fully present, in a mindful spirit. Once you consider a stressful situation with beginner's mind—with curiosity and openness—you might find

43

that the situation is not exactly what you thought it was. Maybe that person didn't mean what you thought he or she meant, or maybe there's another way to look at this conflict. Let go of your negative thoughts and judgments about how the situation "should" be, and experience it just as it is. Practice smiling to the situation or to the other person, with loving-kindness. If you notice self-blame and self-judgment arising, remember to smile to yourself with self-compassion, becoming your own best friend.

—————————————Teen Voices: *Liota*—————————

"Today for the first time I found myself offering myself loving-kindness in a troubling moment. It was such an amazing experience to realize that I could actually want myself to be happy!"

Mindfulness, or "heartfulness," is an unconditional loving presence. With practice, you can learn to meet stress with awareness, curiosity, and compassion. You can become more resilient to stress, tapping into your full powers of strength and wisdom, by inviting your own loving presence into a difficult moment or situation.

Chapter 4

Feeling Your Own Strength: Sitting Like a Mountain

If you want to conquer the anxiety of life,
live in the moment, live in the breath.

— meditation and yoga master Amit Ray

Mindfulness of the breath is the foundation for every single mindfulness practice. Every formal and informal mindfulness practice begins with stopping what you're doing, shifting out of autopilot, getting into the present moment, and enjoying a few mindful breaths.

Mindful breathing isn't hard work. I don't like to call it (as some do) "breath work," or even a "technique." Mindful breathing is just being aware of your body breathing by itself, naturally. Getting in touch with the miracle of life in this way can make breathing very pleasant and enjoyable—a powerful antidote to stress!

✳ Jasmine's Story

I met Jasmine while I was facilitating a mindfulness and stress management workshop for inner-city youth at a community center in Vancouver. Jasmine, though not a participant in the workshop, was struggling with stress and anxiety as she tried to finish school and get a job.

For the first six or eight months I knew Jasmine, I always warmly invited her to join me for the mindfulness workshops. Sometimes, she would decline, saying politely, "No thanks, Dr. Vo—I can't sit still like that. I'm too ADHD!" Other times, she joined the workshop, but, to me, it looked like she wasn't really paying attention—she seemed to be on her cell phone the whole time.

Then, a few months went by that I didn't see her at the community center. When I saw her again, right away she said excitedly, "Dr. Vo, there's something I really want to tell you!"

I smiled at her, happy to see her. "Sure, Jasmine—what's going on?"

She said, "Well, last week, I had to do a medical test. I was hooked up to a bunch of machines. The nurse told me that I needed to relax in order for it to work. I thought I was already relaxed! But she said she could tell I wasn't relaxed, because of the way the machines were reading.

"Then she started getting impatient with me, saying I needed to relax right away or we couldn't do the test. I started freaking out! The more she told me to relax, the more I freaked out… Then I remembered the breathing thing that you taught me. I said to the nurse, 'Wait, just give me a minute—I'm going to do the breathing thing that Dr. Vo taught me!'"

I said, "That's awesome! I'm so glad you remembered. What happened next?"

"Well, I closed my eyes, and I started to breathe. I could hear your voice in my head, the way that you guided the breathing meditations. I just started breathing...I stopped worrying about what might happen next. Before I knew it, the test was done. All this time, it didn't look like I was learning anything from mindfulness, but it was there for me when I needed it!"

Breathing and Smiling

The essence of mindfulness practice can be boiled down to just two words: "breathe" and "smile" (Nhat Hanh 2009, 5). Breathing gets you in touch with the present moment. Smiling opens your mind and heart, allowing you to be fully present to whatever is happening.

When you are feeling happy and enjoying life, there is only one thing to do: breathe and smile.

When you are feeling stressed out, angry, or upset, there is still only one thing to do: breathe and smile.

Now, you may be wondering, *Why should I smile when I'm not feeling happy? Isn't that being fake?* Smiling doesn't necessarily mean pretending to be happy when you're not. Rather, intentionally smiling can help you bring loving-kindness and self-compassion into whatever situation you find yourself in, whether it's an easy situation or a difficult one. When you're in a pleasant situation, smiling can help you enjoy that moment more. When you're in a difficult situation, smiling can remind you to take care of your stress with less judgment and more compassion.

Smiling is like yoga for your face—it relaxes the muscles. And it sends positive signals to your brain. It might sound corny, but smiling really can be healing. Try it!

Try This! Breathe and Smile

Notice how you are feeling right now, in this very moment. Are you feeling calm, relaxed, stressed, agitated, nervous, depressed, angry, or...? Whatever it is that you are experiencing right now, just notice it, without judging it as "good" or "bad."

Remind yourself that, at least for the next few moments, there is nothing else you need to do and nowhere you need to go. Just be fully present right here and right now. That's enough.

Breathe mindfully, following your breath, coming back to the here and now. Intentionally bring a gentle smile to your face, as a reminder to send loving-kindness to yourself. You can say to yourself silently, with each breath, *Breathing in, I know that I am breathing in. Breathing out, I smile. Breathing... Smiling...*

Whatever you experience throughout the day, you can breathe and smile to it. Experiment with this practice, and observe carefully what happens to your body, your emotions, and your thoughts when you train yourself to intentionally breathe and smile.

Just Sitting: Healing from Stress

Do you ever feel as if you're constantly on the go, with barely any time to catch your breath, let alone relax? Do you seem to forever be rushing from school to home, from home to sports practice, from sports practice to work, and from work to hanging out with your friends or family? Is there always too much to do?

Being in "doing" mode all the time activates your stress response and your lizard brain. Allowing yourself some time just to "be" can be very healing. Sitting and meditating means just being yourself, in the present moment. Just sitting and "doing nothing" in this way can be a precious, wonderful gift to yourself. You can let go of your worries, all your thoughts about things that you "have" to do, and all your thoughts about the bad things that have happened to you in the past.

By just sitting, you switch from "doing" to "being." You shift out of autopilot and give your brain and body a chance to rest. Your body is very wise—it already knows how to heal from stress.

When I sit down to meditate, I let go of all my stress about the past and the future, and I just enjoy sitting. This doesn't mean that stress doesn't arise while I am meditating—of course it does! Every time I notice stress arising, however, I just come back to the present moment, back to my breath, with a gentle smile. After a few minutes of sitting like this, I feel a transformation in myself. I feel lighter, as though a weight has been lifted from my shoulders, because I'm no longer trying to be or do anything in particular. Sitting meditation becomes a

49

great source of joy for me. You can give yourself this same gift: a precious opportunity to just be yourself.

Sitting Like a Mountain

When I look at a mountain, I see how solid and stable it is, firmly rooted in the earth, as it rises toward the sky. I also notice its quiet dignity. The mountain doesn't have to shout, "Hey, look at me!" The mountain just sits there, majestically.

You can be like that mountain. You can embody those qualities that we often see in a beautiful mountain—stability, quietude, dignity. You don't need to do anything special. Just sit and be present with your breath and your body.

Sitting and Breathing with Whatever Arises

Despite what you might have heard, meditation isn't something that requires a lot of effort. When you sit down to meditate, know that there is no problem for you to solve, nothing for you to fix. There is nothing much you need to do at all. You don't even need to try to get rid of stress or feel more relaxed. Just allow yourself to be, accepting yourself fully, just as you are, right now.

Once you sit down and start to pay attention to your own sensations, feelings, and thoughts, perhaps you will find peace, relaxation, and happiness. If just sitting and breathing feels good, you can smile and enjoy it. If stress or pain arises, you don't have to push it away or "fix" it in any way. You can just sit with it, observing it with openness and curiosity, and holding it gently for the moment. Your breath can be your "home base," your anchor. No matter how confused or lost you feel, your breath is always there for you. You can practice sitting meditation anytime, anywhere, whether you're feeling calm or stressed. Whatever storm is raging inside of you, you can breathe with it, touching some peace with each breath.

Sometimes, when difficult feelings or thoughts are present, it may seem too hard for you to sit still. That's okay. You'll learn other ways to handle difficulty—ones that don't involve sitting still—later in this book. That said, sitting meditation is still a great foundation for other mindfulness strategies, so I hope you'll experiment with it, with a spirit of openness and curiosity.

Try This! Sitting Meditation

You can do this mindfulness practice using the instructions below or with the help of the recording (track 3) available at http://www.newharbinger .com/30802. I recommend that you start by following along with the recording a few times. Then, try it without the recording, guiding yourself with your own inner voice. If you will be practicing without the aid of the recording, you may wish to set a timer (perhaps on your phone) for three minutes, or five minutes, or ten minutes—however long you wish to meditate.

First, find a place to sit. A quiet room or corner should work well. If there is noise or if there are people nearby, that's okay too. You might ask the people around you to not disturb you, if you can. You may also wish to turn off your phone and any other electronics.

If you are sitting on a chair, allow your sit bones to connect firmly with the chair, and your feet to rest flat on the floor.

If you are sitting on the floor, use a cushion or pillow that is tall enough and firm enough to provide good support. You can kneel on the cushion, with your knees bent in front of you (with your sit bones resting on your heels). Or you can sit with your legs crossed. Find a comfortable position in which your body feels at ease.

Maintain an upright but relaxed position. Imagine yourself as a mountain, tall and dignified, in a quiet and relaxed kind of way. Your upper body should be straight, but not stiff. Experiment with leaning forward and backward a tiny bit, and also side to side, until you find your body's natural upright position, in which your spine supports the weight of your body and your body holds itself up.

If you feel comfortable closing your eyes, go ahead and close your eyes. If you would rather keep your eyes open, that's okay too. Just gaze softly (without focusing on anything in particular) at the floor in front of you.

Tell yourself that for however long you have chosen to meditate, you have nowhere to go and nothing else to do. You can let go of the past; you can let go of the future. Allow yourself to just be fully present right here and now.

Become aware of your body in the sitting position. Bring your awareness to your feet touching the floor and the chair beneath you (if you are in a chair). How does your upper body feel? Are you slouching, or are you sitting upright? How do your head and neck feel? You don't need to sit perfectly still, like a statue. Simply notice what is happening, with an attitude of friend-liness toward your body, and make any adjustment that is appropriate for your body in this moment.

Bring your awareness to your breath going in and out of your body. Just notice your breath doing what it does naturally—don't try to change it or control it.

Breathe in. Follow your in-breath from the beginning, to the middle, to the end.

Breathe out. Follow your out-breath from the beginning, to the middle, to the end.

You may wish to say silently to yourself, *Breathing in, I know that I am breathing in. Breathing out, I know that I am breathing out. In… Out…*

Experiment with smiling as you sit in meditation, as in the "Breathe and Smile" practice. *Breathing in, I know that I am breathing in. Breathing out, I smile. Breathing… Smiling…*

Hold in your awareness whatever arises. You might experience difficult thoughts, uncomfortable sensations, or negative emotions. You don't need to change anything or try to force this experience of meditation to be a certain way. Whatever it is you are experiencing, as best you can, just notice it. Allow it to be there, with an attitude of kindness and curiosity.

If you find yourself becoming distracted or overwhelmed, or lost or confused, that's okay. It isn't possible for anyone to keep his or her awareness on the breath 100 percent of the time. Noticing that your mind wandered is in fact a good thing, because it means that you are mindful of "mind-wandering." So simply notice whenever your mind has wandered and then gently bring your attention back to your breath. Any time you feel lost or confused, just bring your attention back to your breath. *Breathing in, I know that I am breathing in. Breathing out, I know that I am breathing out. In… Out…*

Notice what happens now that you are intentionally stopped, sitting still, and doing nothing. If it feels pleasant, can you just appreciate and enjoy that, without clinging to that feeling? If it feels awkward or boring or weird, can you just notice that and keep doing nothing?

You don't need to try too hard with this practice. You don't need to try to have a certain experience, accomplish or achieve anything in particular, or change the way that you feel. Whatever you are experiencing—whatever this meditation is like for you—is okay.

As best you can, invite an attitude of self-compassion to your meditation practice. Sitting meditation is not a chore or punishment, and it doesn't need to hurt. If you notice your feet are falling asleep, your leg is tingling, or other parts of your body are beginning to hurt, try just paying attention to that sensation for three breaths, continuing to smile. Then, if you need to move or adjust your position, do it slowly, with careful attention, continuing to follow your in-breath and your out-breath. If you need to get up, stretch, or walk around mindfully, that's okay too.

When the timer goes off or when you wish to end the meditation, open your eyes if they were closed. Take a moment to stretch, shake out your body, and massage your arms or legs if they feel stiff. Thank yourself for taking the time to take good care of your body and mind with mindfulness and compassion.

The Benefits of Daily Mindfulness Practice

Daily mindfulness practice can literally change the brain, in ways that researchers can see on MRI scans! Daily mindfulness practice can actually "rewire" your brain, strengthening the connections between your human brain and your lizard brain and making you more resilient when faced with stress. It's almost like doing brain surgery, but without the surgery!

You could also think of regular mindfulness practice as kind of like going to the gym and working out often. If you went to the gym and lifted weights just once, what do you think would happen? Maybe your muscles would be sore for a day or two, but you probably wouldn't notice any increase in muscle size or strength. If you went to the gym and lifted weights every day, on the other hand, what would happen? You would find that your muscles got bigger and stronger, whether that was your intention or not.

Practicing mindfulness every day is like working out your "mindfulness muscle." The more you practice, the stronger that "muscle" gets, whether or not you realize it right away. The more you meditate, the better your ability to handle stress and difficulty will be, and the more confidence you will have in that ability.

I'm not saying that you have to sit and meditate for an hour every day. In fact, mindfulness practice is probably most helpful in small, but frequent, doses. It's like brushing your teeth at least twice a day—you spend just a few minutes every day on dental hygiene, for the sake of your dental health. Daily mindfulness practice is like "mental hygiene," for the sake of your mental health.

So, I invite you to give mindfulness practice a try for just a few minutes every day for the next eight weeks. You may have the thought that meditation is stupid or is never going to work for you—alternatively, you may think meditation is great or is going to solve all your problems. Regardless of how you feel about it now or over the next eight weeks, just let go of all your expectations and treat meditation as an experiment, with an attitude of beginner's mind.

I recommend that you meditate at the same time every day. You can start with just three to five minutes of mindful sitting and breathing. A good time for you to meditate might be in the morning, before you brush your teeth. Or, it might be at night, before you go to bed. Keep it up every day, even if it feels weird or boring, just to see what happens.

Just as you shouldn't wait until you have a cavity to start brushing your teeth, you shouldn't wait until you're stressed to start meditating. With just a few minutes of daily mindfulness practice, you can help your body start to heal from stress and build resilience. But don't take my word for it. Give it a try, and see what happens.

✱ *John's Story*

John said he suffered from constant stress and anxiety. He felt stressed and worried at home, at school, and even when he was out with his friends.

When I first led the class in a sitting meditation, John said he had a really hard time with it. He felt anxious, nervous, and fidgety, as if he had to get up and move all the time. He also had a strong urge to check his phone, even though everyone was supposed to have their phones off during class. He said, "I just can't sit still."

In the next couple of classes, John actually got up and walked around in the middle of a ten-minute sitting meditation. After a few weeks, however, he was able to sit still and follow his breath for the entire practice. By the end of the eight-week course, he reported that just sitting quietly and doing nothing was a great relief from stress: "Sitting meditation helps me chill out and clear my head." He even suggested that we try sitting for longer periods in class!

Sitting meditation allows you to experience the joy and peace that is available to you in the present moment. It is a quiet celebration of life. If you sit and pay attention, you will become deeply aware of being alive in the here and now. You will notice that your lungs are filling with air, bringing oxygen to nourish every cell in your body. Being alive is a miracle. This breath is a miracle. Sitting is a miracle. The only way to touch this miracle is by being present and paying careful attention. Right now is the only time you have to be alive.

Chapter 5

Embracing the Now

Do every act of your life as though it were
the very last act of your life.

— second-century Roman emperor
Marcus Aurelius Antoninus

When you are stressed out, you might spend a lot of time
thinking about the past or worrying about the future. You
might have a lot of judgments about the way things "should"
or "shouldn't" be. If you don't know how to handle stress,
you can easily get carried away by these kinds of thoughts
until you have completely lost touch with what is happening
around you—in other words, until your mind is miles away
from your body.

In this chapter, you will learn to tame your lizard brain and
handle stress by coming back to the present moment, living
each moment as if it was the most important moment in your
entire life.

✳ *Rose's Story*

Rose said that although she loved school and she loved to learn, she had a really hard time taking quizzes and exams. Sometimes when she sat down to take an exam, she said, she would get so stressed out that her brain "froze," and she couldn't think at all.

For example, one morning, Rose sat down to take a science exam. Although she had studied hard, in her moment of stress she couldn't remember what she had learned. She left the science room thinking, I did really badly on that exam. What's wrong with me? *That afternoon, she went to her dance class, which was something she usually loved. But she was in such a bad mood from earlier that she couldn't get into her warm-up routine. Suddenly, she realized,* I've been thinking about that exam all day long! But the exam is in the past—I don't need to keep thinking about it and stressing about it. *She decided to let go of her thoughts and worries about the exam and just be fully in the present moment. As she told us, "I decided to be more present for dancing. I ended up enjoying the dance class a lot more since I wasn't thinking about school the whole time. And, my mood was a lot better by the end."*

Freeing Yourself from the Past and the Future

Perhaps something really difficult happened to you in the past—maybe you were abused, treated very badly, or hurt by someone you trusted. Maybe the stress and pain from those experiences are still present in your body and mind. With mindfulness, you can take care of those old wounds, right here in the present moment. You don't have to dwell on the past, replaying difficult memories over and over again. You also don't have to run away from the past or try to push those difficult memories away. No matter what has happened in your life, you possess the wisdom and strength to heal from it. You were born with this strength, and no one and nothing can take it away from you.

Sometimes, instead of being caught in the past, you might be stressed about the future. For example, you might wonder, *How am I going to finish all the homework I have to do tonight? Or What if other kids make fun of me tomorrow?* Regrets about the past and worries about the future can pull you away from the present moment, activate your lizard brain, and lead to more stress. You can let go of that stress by breathing mindfully and coming back to the present moment.

Freeing Yourself from Judgments

Any time you are stressed, judgmental thinking only worsens that stress. Mindfulness involves freeing yourself from your judgments—judgments about what is good or bad, judgments about what is right or wrong, judgments about the situation, and especially judgments about yourself. One common kind of judgment involves wishing things were not the way they are. Such wishes often hold someone up to blame—for example, *I wish he hadn't done that* or *I wish she would stop doing this*. Judgmental thoughts sometimes also contain the word "shouldn't" or "can't." For example, *He shouldn't be saying that. What's wrong with him?* Or *I can't stand it when my mom doesn't let me go out on weekends*. Often, our harshest judgments are about ourselves—for example, *I'm too fat* or *I'm so stupid*.

Judgments get in the way of being deeply in touch with the present moment. Thoughts like *I need things to be different; I'm not okay with how things are* create a battle between your mind and your reality. This mental battle activates the fight, flight, or freeze response in your lizard brain, increasing your stress.

If you pay close attention to your thoughts throughout the day, you might be surprised at how often judgmental thoughts arise. You can free yourself from judgments, and all the stress that comes with them, by coming back to the present moment with an open heart and an attitude of acceptance. The ancient Chinese philosopher Lao-tzu said, "Be content with what you have; rejoice in the way things are. When you realize there is nothing lacking, the whole world belongs to you" (2006, 44). With mindfulness, you can become 100 percent present with the moment *just as it is*, instead of as you *wish* it was. Letting go of judgment sends a powerful message to your lizard brain: *It's okay—there's no need to fight.*

Nonjudgment is sometimes misunderstood as passiveness or apathy. Let me be clear about one thing: nonjudging doesn't mean ignoring problems or injustices. In fact, with beginner's mind and an open heart, you'll actually be able to see difficult situations more clearly. Any time you do need to take action in an unfair situation, openness and flexibility will help you be more creative and effective. You'll be bringing mindful understanding and compassion into a difficult situation, instead of acting from a place of blame and judgment and perhaps making things worse. Later in this book, you'll learn how to practice mindfulness in many difficult situations.

This Is It

You can't change the past. You can't escape the present moment. And you can't live in the future because it hasn't arrived yet. Don't allow yourself to be pulled away from the present moment. Don't rob yourself of the peace and happiness that is available in the here and now.

You may be waiting for something that you think will make you happy—like graduating from high school or college or finding the perfect boyfriend or girlfriend. Having hopes for your future is wonderful, and I'm not saying that you should never plan or never think about the future. But don't wait to start enjoying life. As you plan, be *aware* that you are planning. Remember to enjoy the journey in the present moment. The best way to create a positive future is to take really good care of yourself and the people around you, right here and now.

Learn to get deeply in touch with the present moment, and recognize the healing power of simple experiences—such as looking at the big, blue sky; feeling a gentle breeze on your face; or receiving a smile from your little brother—that are available to you right here and now. Whatever you are looking for, look for it right here and now. If you are looking for happiness, look for it right here and now. If you are looking for relief from past hurts, you will find that only right here and now.

The present moment is the only moment that you have. This very moment is the most important moment of your life. You can start enjoying life right now, with this breath. And this breath. And this breath… This is it.

Try This! "This Is It"

The next time your mind is far away in time or space, simply notice that your thoughts are somewhere other than the here and now. Then ask yourself, *What was I just thinking about? Where did my mind go to?* Maybe your mind was in the past, dwelling on something difficult that happened to you. Maybe your mind was in the future, worrying about something that might or might not happen. Or maybe you were thinking about something that you think you need to have before you can be happy.

Guess what? As soon as you noticed you were being pulled away from the present moment, you entered a moment of mindfulness!

Congratulate yourself for noticing that your mind wandered. Then remind yourself, *This is it! Right here, right now.* Gently return to the present moment, using your breath as your anchor. Follow your in-breath and your out-breath for a few breaths. Bring a gentle smile to your lips. Then, return to what you were doing, but continue to follow your breath, and continue to touch the present moment.

Ask yourself, *What is happening right now? And right* now? *And right* now?

"Tuning In": Dealing with Distractions

It's human nature to try to distract yourself from uncomfortable feelings, like worry, loneliness, or sadness. And there are so many ways to distract yourself—from your cell phone, to the Internet, to video games, to TV. Sometimes these distractions can seem irresistible. It can seem so tempting to play video games or surf the Internet for hours and hours.

Sometimes, distractions can be healthy—for example, when you take a break from homework by going for a walk with your dog or calling up your best friend to talk about something fun. But sometimes, distractions can be an attempt to escape or "tune out" from life, or to cover up uncomfortable feelings. A distraction can even become an addiction, something you can't "put down" even when you want to. At that point, it's not even fun anymore. Instead, it keeps you awake all night, interferes with your life at home and at school, and ends up causing more stress. For many teens, this is what happens with technology. I'm not saying that you should never use technology, because it can be great for having fun, learning, and connecting with others. But can you notice if and when you're using technology in order to tune out from reality? And can you observe, with self-compassion, what it is inside yourself that you may be attempting to cover up?

Maybe you sometimes tune out or distract yourself in ways that you know can be dangerous and harmful, like cutting yourself, using drugs, or drinking alcohol. If you can learn to stay present with uncomfortable feelings, then you can learn to handle stress better. With mindfulness, you can train yourself to stay present, to stay awake to reality. You can "tune in" and show up for life rather than tuning out and trying to escape. Just as you can't properly heal from a wound unless you attend to it and care for it, you can't properly heal from stress and pain unless you fully tune in to life, courageously and openheartedly, one moment at a time.

Mindfulness and Gratitude

For me personally, mindfulness practice boils down to two things: first, the art of joyful living—learning to enjoy my life more deeply, more fully—second, the art of handling stress. Just like you and everyone else, I sometimes experience stress. With mindfulness, I know how to handle it so that I don't get overwhelmed.

It turns out that joyful living and handling stress go hand in hand. Any time I'm enjoying my life—for whatever reason—I find I can handle stress much better. Mindfulness helps me enjoy the "good stuff." And mindfulness helps me handle stress without fighting it or making it worse. Mindfulness helps me be open to whatever comes my way, whether I might consider it "good" or "bad."

We'll come back to handling stress later in this book. For now, let's see how a mindfulness practice might help you enjoy life, or notice the good stuff, more. Being aware of and grateful for the positive things in your life can help you heal from the effects of stress.

Try This! Gratitude

Take a moment to become aware of one or two things that you can be grateful for, like things that are fun or things that you have enjoyed lately. They can be big things (like winning an award or championship) or little things (like petting your cat this morning). They can be things that you notice right now, things from earlier today, or things from earlier this week. What are a few of the good things, the pleasant moments, the positive events? Even if you are under a lot of stress right now, can you identify just one or two little things in your life that you are grateful for? Don't judge yourself too much if it is hard to think of anything.

What did you come up with? If you found it difficult to think of anything positive in your life, maybe you can identify with one or more of the following things that teens have told me they are grateful for.

- "Being on the soccer team."

- "Seeing my best friend."

- "My family."

- "My coach."

- "The sun was shining this morning."

- "Riding my bike."

Having read this list, can you think of any more things in your own life that you are grateful for?

Enjoying the Little Things

When you pay close attention to each moment, you can start to see the small wonders of life. Maybe the sky is a fabulous shade of blue today. Maybe your best friend's smile warms your heart. There are wonders in every moment, just waiting for you to be present and recognize them. Maybe if you pay close attention, it feels good just to breathe. The cool air entering your lungs—how wonderful that can feel, like a glass of cool water on a hot day! Even when things are stressful in your life, this very breath can be a small moment of joy. Just by paying attention to your breath, you might feel grateful to be alive, grateful that your lungs are working and that you have air to breathe.

Be careful, however, to not get too attached to whatever it is you're enjoying. Perhaps you have a tendency to want to hold on to happy moments, wishing every moment could be like that. But every moment can't be happy, and, in hard times, wishing for things to be different than the way they are will only increase your suffering. With mindfulness, you can breathe in and enjoy, then breathe out and let go. You don't need to hold on to anything. Each breath heralds a new moment—and, perhaps, something new to enjoy. You can practice mindfulness in this way anytime, no matter where you are.

Try This! Mindfulness of Pleasant Events

Over the next few days, pay attention to the small pleasant moments in your life. When you notice a pleasant moment, smile and allow a pleasant emotion like happiness or gratitude to arise.

Experiencing a pleasant emotion is like having your best friend come over for a visit. Recognize your pleasant emotion. Enjoy it while it lasts. When it starts to fade, let it go. You don't need to try to hold on to happiness, just as you wouldn't force your best friend to stay any longer than he or she wanted to. Just breathe again, smile again, and open your mind and heart to the next moment, whatever arises.

Here is a short saying from Thich Nhat Hanh (1993, 15) that I use to help myself practice mindfulness of pleasant events. You can try it, too. Any time you notice a small pleasant moment in your life, say silently to yourself:

- *Breathing in, I know this is a pleasant moment.*

- *Breathing out, I smile.*

- *Pleasant moment.*

- *Smiling.*

Try This! Keep a Gratitude and Mindfulness Journal

At the end of each day, write down something in your life that you are grateful for. It could be a person in your life. It could be something that happened during your day. It can be something big or something small. As you think about what you are grateful for, breathe mindfully in and out three times, and bring your awareness to any feeling of gratitude that arises. Notice what is present in your body—for example, a warm sensation in your heart. Does the thought of what you are grateful for bring a gentle smile to your lips?

If it helps, as you notice these pleasant moments, practice saying to yourself silently, *Breathing in, I know this is a pleasant moment. Breathing out, I smile. Pleasant moment… Smiling…*

Developing a Daily Mindfulness Practice

What benefits have you noticed already as you practice mindfulness? Can you think of any possible benefits to continuing to practice mindful breathing for a few minutes every day, on good days as well as bad days? Are there any challenges that might keep you from practicing it regularly? Can you think of some ways to work with those challenges?

Remember that mindfulness is simple, but it's not always easy. Remind yourself that daily mindfulness practice is like exercising your mindfulness muscle or practicing mental hygiene. Just like lifting weights to build muscle and strength, practicing mindfulness might not yield dramatic results right away. But if you keep at it patiently and gently, you might notice after a few days or a few weeks that you feel a little less stressed or a little happier.

You might find it difficult to keep up your daily practice, however. You might ask yourself, *Why should I keep doing this? What's the point?* Or thoughts like *This isn't working* or *I'm too busy—I don't have time to meditate* may arise. Even if you don't believe that practicing mindfulness is having any positive effects—even if you think, *It's not working*—your brain might be growing and developing in ways that you can't recognize right away. Whether you feel as if it's working or not, continue to experiment with mindfulness for a few more weeks. See what happens if you just stick with it every day, as best you can, whether you feel like it or not. That said, mindfulness shouldn't feel like a burden, a chore, or more "homework" that you have to do. Try to invite a sense of lightheartedness, joy, and playfulness into your daily practice. Let go of expectations about what's "supposed" to happen. By simply sticking with it, and staying curious, you might discover new and surprising possibilities.

Chapter 6

Caring for Your Body: The Body Scan

Mindfulness is simply being aware of what is happening right now without wishing it were different; enjoying the pleasant without holding on when it changes (which it will); being with the unpleasant without fearing it will always be this way (which it won't).

— meditation teacher James Baraz (2007)

Stress doesn't just affect your mind—it affects your body. Whenever you are stressed, your body becomes tense. You might experience that stress in the form of a "tension headache," a "gut feeling," an aching in your shoulders, a pain in your back, or problems eating or sleeping. Bringing mindfulness and self-compassion to your body can help you release and heal from the stress that lives in your body. Since your body and mind are deeply connected, releasing stress in your body will also release stress in your mind.

Our bodies carry so much wisdom. The sensations you feel in your body are important messages about your health, your stress levels, and your relationships. For example, you might find that your heart feels lighter in the presence of someone you love. On the other hand, an ache in your stomach might be a sign of stress or anxiety about something going on in your life. Even basic signals like hunger or sleepiness tell you how you can take good care of your body and mind.

For one reason or another, you may currently be out of touch with your body, having forgotten how to listen to it. With mindful awareness, you can learn how to tune back in and make wise use of the messages coming from your body.

Teen Voices: *Jasmine*

"Practicing mindfulness can be very difficult, especially the first several times. However, once your body has learned to accept the present moment for how it is, without judgment, it becomes easier. When I first started to practice mindfulness, I was skeptical that it would benefit me or help me in any way, but I still decided to give it a try. I went in with an open mind, and I started to notice sensations in my body that I never knew were there. Over the course of a few weeks, I learned how powerful our bodies are. They give us signals when we are feeling anxious and overwhelmed, or when we are feeling pleasant emotions such as happiness or excitement."

The Body Scan: Tuning In to Your Body

One way to get back in touch with your body is a meditation called the body scan, in which you bring mindful awareness, loving-kindness, and self-compassion to your body, one body part at a time. The body scan is a true act of love for your body. It gives your body the gift of time, rest, and compassionate attention. As you invite the energy of mindfulness into your body, you give your body a chance to heal from stress and pain. Because your body and your mind are deeply connected, as you heal your body, you are also healing your mind. Getting back into your body also helps you let go of stressful thoughts. (You'll learn more about how to let go of stressful thoughts in chapter 9.)

The body scan is one of my favorite formal mindfulness practices. I love to practice the body scan at night before I go to sleep. I also sometimes practice it at the end of a really stressful day when I feel pain and exhaustion in my body. I also like to practice a "mini body scan" on a chair in my office any time I have five or ten minutes to close my eyes and rest.

The purpose of the body scan is not necessarily to relax or to go to sleep, although it can help with that sometimes. The intent of the body scan is to help you awaken to sensations in your body, in the present moment. If the body scan is relaxing for you, wonderful. If not, it is still a great mindfulness practice. If you fall asleep while practicing the body scan, that's okay. The important thing is that you stay open and curious to your body's experience.

Try This! The Body Scan

You can do this mindfulness practice using the instructions below or with the help of the recording (track 4) available at http://www.newharbinger .com/30802. *If you will be using the recording, you can practice the body scan while lying on a mat or bed. If you don't have a place to lie down, or if you will be reading from the book, you can also practice the body scan while sitting on a chair or even standing.*

If you will be lying down for this practice, lie flat on your back. Place your feet slightly apart, letting your toes fall to the sides. Place your arms by your sides, palms up. If you want to, bend your knees slightly. Close your eyes, if that feels comfortable. Bring your awareness to the sensation of lying on the mat or bed.

Tell yourself that in this moment, you have nothing else to do and nowhere to go. You can simply allow yourself to be present, just as you are.

Connect with your breath. Your breath is the bridge that brings your body and mind together in the present moment. If it helps, say silently to yourself, *Breathing in, I know that I am breathing in. Breathing out, I know that I am breathing out. In… Out…*

Bring your awareness to your body, starting with your left foot. As you breathe in, imagine that you are breathing in through your left foot, all the way up your body, to your lungs. As you breathe out, imagine that you are breathing out all the way through your body, through your left leg and out through your left foot. What sensations are you noticing in your left foot right now? Can you feel your toes? Can you feel the bottom of your foot? Can you feel the sock around your foot, if there is one? Do you feel warmth, or do you feel coolness? Do you feel any tiredness, tension, or pain? Is there any tingling or numbness? Are you getting a sense of strength, comfort, and health? If you are experiencing no sensation, just notice that.

Breathe and smile to your left foot. Say to yourself silently, *Breathing in, I am aware of my left foot. Breathing out, I smile to my left foot. Aware of left foot… Smiling to left foot…* Breathing brings awareness to your foot. Smiling is an act of kindness and compassion for your foot.

With the next breath in, gather your awareness. With the next breath out, shift your awareness slowly to your left ankle, noticing any sensations there. As you continue to breathe mindfully, bring your awareness up your leg to your calf, your shin, and your knee. Notice sensations in your left upper leg and left hip. In the same way that you breathed and smiled to your left foot, bring awareness, care, and curiosity to your left leg. *Breathing in, I am aware of my left leg. Breathing out, I smile to my left leg. Aware of left leg… Smiling…*

Bring the same awareness, care, and curiosity to your entire body, one part at a time. Anchor yourself in your breath, and bring that mindful and cleansing breath through each part of your body. By being curious and gentle with the moment-to-moment sensations in each part of your body, you are allowing your body to rest and to release any stress that is present there. Focus for at least three breaths on each body part. If you have more time, you can give yourself two or three minutes on each body part. There is no "right" or "wrong" way to do this practice, but here is the order in which I myself like to work through the parts of the body:

1. Left foot

2. Left leg

3. Right foot

4. Right leg

5. Abdomen and belly

6. Upper body, chest, and shoulders

7. Back

8. Hands and arms

9. Head and face

After scanning the last body part, gather your awareness one last time as you breathe in, and bring your awareness to your body as a whole. As you breathe out, allow your whole body to breathe.

Then, check in with your body: What is the state of your body now? Is it the same as, or different than, when you started the body scan? Are there any parts of your body that still feel stressed or tense or that need extra care? What about your emotions and your stress level? Are they the same as when you started, or are they different in any way? Take a few seconds to notice what is arising, what is changing from moment to moment.

Wake up your body. Feel free to wiggle your toes and your fingers. Open your eyes, if they were closed. Slowly—there's no need to rush—sit up, and return your attention to your surroundings.

Thank yourself for taking the time to take care of your body, aware that you just practiced an act of self-compassion. Then, carry on with your day, mindfully.

Handling Pain and Discomfort: Not Turning Away

For many teens, stress and physical pain are two sides of the same coin. Chronic stress can become toxic to your body. You might experience stress as chronic pain—for example, daily headaches or chronic abdominal pain or back pain. Some teens also have health conditions or injuries that can cause or contribute to chronic pain. Whatever the cause, chronic pain can be very stressful, and it can eventually lead to depression or anxiety. Pain can cause stress, stress can worsen pain, and you can end up getting caught in a vicious cycle. The good news is you can get out of this cycle by learning how to handle physical pain and discomfort with wisdom.

You might think that "pain" and "suffering" are the same thing. But pain is just a sensation. Suffering is a result of your relationship with that sensation. For example, a mother once told me that when she gave birth to her daughter, she was in a lot of physical pain, but she didn't suffer. She explained, "I breathed, and I embraced the pain."

Pain is inevitable. Suffering is, at least to some extent, optional. Mindfulness can help you reduce your suffering, even as you experience pain. Here is a helpful equation to remember:

$$Suffering = Pain \times Resistance$$

Here are some ways that you might resist pain, perhaps without intending to or even realizing it:

* Judgmental thinking: *This is horrible; I can't stand it;* or *What's wrong with me?*

* Pretending that the pain isn't there: *No, it doesn't hurt—everything is fine!*

* Resistance in your body: clenching your teeth, tensing your body

* Trying to numb or "cover up" the pain with alcohol, drugs, or other unhealthy distractions

Resisting pain might work for a while, but usually the pain doesn't go away for long. In fact, resisting pain can actually make the pain last longer and feel worse. As psychologists sometimes say, "What you resist, persists." For example, bracing yourself against pain tenses the muscles in your body, which can amplify the pain. Worrying and being afraid of pain can actually increase the pain and worsen your suffering.

With mindfulness, you can uncover and examine your own tendencies to resist pain. Then, you can make a mindful choice to relate to pain in a radically different way and, perhaps, suffer less. Instead of turning away from pain, you can actually "turn toward" your pain, with a spirit of gentleness and compassion. You can accept your pain, just as it is. I'm not saying that you have to *like* your pain. But you *can* make peace with your pain and, in doing so, let go of the extra stress and suffering that comes from fighting and resisting it. You can even recognize and make peace with your dislike of the pain—with your tendency to resist it—with awareness and self-compassion. This can be profoundly liberating: once you know that you don't have to be afraid of pain, you will let go of a huge amount of stress.

You may even find that your experience of the pain changes, or perhaps it isn't quite what you thought it was.

✳ *Rapinder's Story*

Rapinder shared that he suffered from chronic pain throughout his whole body. He had been to many doctors, and medications didn't seem to help him very much. At the beginning of the MARS-A course, Rapinder said, "I'm always in pain. It's constant and nonstop." Once he started to pay attention mindfully to the pain, however, he was surprised to find that his assessment had been inaccurate. He reported, "Sometimes the pain goes up, sometimes it goes down, and there was even a moment yesterday when I 'tuned in' and noticed that the pain was actually pretty low."

Everything I am saying here about handling physical pain applies equally to handling emotional pain. We'll talk more about handling difficult emotions in chapter 10.

Try This! Handling Pain and Discomfort with the Body Scan

Using the body scan, you can train yourself to breathe and make peace with, even embrace, your pain. The next time you practice the body scan, spend a little extra time bringing mindfulness to the parts of your body in which you are experiencing pain (or discomfort, stress, or tension). Follow these steps:

1. **Investigate the sensations.** It takes a lot of courage to investigate your pain. As best you can, notice and accept the pain. Stay present with it compassionately for as long as you can. Remain open, curious, and kind toward this sensation to the best of your

ability, even though it's uncomfortable or unpleasant. Remember that you are strong enough to be with yourself and be with your pain.

Observe the pain closely, with curiosity. Is it the same from one moment to the next, or is it changing? Can you continue to breathe with it?

2. **Observe your thoughts and emotions.** Staying in the present moment, allow your awareness to broaden. What else is present for you right now, in addition to the pain? Are you noticing any tendency to resist the pain—to avoid it, deny it, or push it away? Is your mind being pulled away from the present moment into the past or the future? What stories is your mind creating about the pain? For example, *The pain is never going to go away.* Or *I can't wait until the pain is gone.*

    Also notice what emotions seem to come with the pain. Is there fear? Anger? Sadness?

    Are these thoughts and emotions useful to you? Or are they increasing your suffering? What can you discover about your own tendencies to resist pain? How can you mindfully change your relationship with pain?

    Notice, without judgment, the thoughts and stories and emotions that arise. Let go of your thoughts and judgments by coming back to your breath. Shift from thinking *about* the pain to simply experiencing the sensation of it *directly* in your body. You may need to do this over and over again.

3. **Establish a wise relationship with the pain.** Experience the pain one moment at a time. Remind yourself that you are more than your pain, just as when a storm comes, the clear blue sky is still there above the clouds. When pain is present for you, you still have your

mindful breathing, and you still have that mindful, peaceful place inside of you that you can tap into anytime. Instead of rejecting or turning away from pain, experiment with turning *toward* it. Experiment with breathing into it, little by little, breath by breath. The peace that comes with mindful breathing can help you stay present with the pain. *Yes,* you can tell yourself, *pain is here. But, my breathing and mindfulness are also here, to help me embrace the pain and to hold it with compassionate awareness.*

If it helps, during your meditation, say to yourself, *Breathing in, I am aware of my pain. Breathing out, I smile to my pain. Aware of pain... Smiling...* This practice is a reminder to smile and be gentle with yourself.

✳ *Penny's Story*

Penny had had back pain for many years, and medications didn't seem to help very much. One week she shared that, since our last meeting, she had decided to make use of her new knowledge that Suffering = Pain x Resistance. She explained, "My usual focus in the past has been how to get rid of pain and not feel it. This week, I tried not to resist it. Instead, I tried to explore it, just let it be there. For example, I described it to myself, trying to understand it as best I could, and not fight against it."

I asked her, "How has the pain changed?"

She replied, "My pain hasn't changed very much. But, I'm suffering a lot less, and my mind in particular is suffering a lot less!"

Continuing Your Daily Practice: Mindfulness of Your Body

Try practicing the body scan for five to ten minutes every day for the next week. Find a time and place that work for you—maybe before you go to bed or when you get home from school—and stick to this routine. You can practice for longer—say, twenty or thirty minutes—on the weekend if you have time. (Track 11 at http://www.newharbinger.com/30802 is a long version of the body scan.) Or try alternating the formal practices you have learned so far: do the body scan one day and sitting meditation the next. After you've practiced the body scan a few times using a recording, experiment with guiding yourself through the body scan silently, without the recording.

Mindfulness of your body will help you tune in to your body's important messages. It can also help you handle physical pain and discomfort. Instead of being ruled by these sensations, you can learn to take care of them with compassion. The French philosopher Jean-Paul Sartre said, "Freedom is what you do with what has been done to you." Handling pain with awareness is true liberation and true healing. It takes time and practice, but I am sure that you can succeed!

Chapter 7

Everyday Mindfulness: Finding Freedom Wherever You Are

It's about being in the moment. All we have is the moment.
There's no past, there's no future—it's the moment. That's it.

— jazz legend Sonny Rollins

So far in this book, we've talked mostly about formal mindfulness practices, like sitting meditation and the body scan. Formal mindfulness involves taking time out of your day just to meditate. It can be two minutes, five minutes, or thirty minutes.

You might be thinking, *I'm too busy—when am I supposed to find the time for that?* The good news is even if you can't set aside any time specifically for mindfulness, the joy of mindfulness is available to you in every moment of every day, in any activity that you are doing.

Washing the Dishes

I had my first real meditation experience while on a three-week meditation retreat at Plum Village, a meditation center in the beautiful countryside of southern France. The first day I was there, I was looking forward to just chilling out, but one of the meditation teachers assigned me to something called "working meditation." My "meditation" was to wash the dishes in the kitchen after dinner. He explained, "Washing the dishes is just as much of a meditation as sitting in the meditation hall. When you wash the dishes, don't wash the dishes just to hurry and finish, so that you can be free to do something else. Wash the dishes just to wash the dishes. Wash each dish as if it is the most important thing to do in the entire world."

When I heard that, I felt irritated. I thought, *What do you mean, work? I'm on vacation right now. I came here to meditate, not work!* That first evening, I wasn't very mindful as I washed the dishes. I thought, *I can't wait to finish this so I can go do something else*. Washing the dishes was not very fun!

Nonetheless, I kept practicing "dishwashing meditation" throughout the week. I began following my breath as I washed the dishes. I began to pay closer attention to the sounds and smells around me. I began to enjoy the warmth of the water on my hands and the feeling of soapsuds between my fingers. At some point, the boring activity of washing dishes started to become really interesting; it didn't feel like a chore anymore. I learned that any activity can be a meditation. Now, to this very day, I truly enjoy washing dishes, and I find it a very peaceful and enjoyable mindfulness practice.

Informal Mindfulness: Don't Wait—Meditate!

Informal mindfulness involves bringing mindful awareness into everyday, routine activities that you already do. Being mindful as you simply go about your day can be a source of joy as well as stress relief. Any time you are sitting, you can follow your breath, smile, and come home to the present moment. You can practice doing this while sitting on the bus, sitting in a car, or sitting in the classroom. You can also bring this same mindful awareness to any other activity of daily life. You can touch the present moment deeply as you brush your teeth in the morning. You can let go of stress by being mindful as you put on your clothes, tie your shoes, or walk to class.

Perhaps you have a tendency to try to do two, three, or even four things at the same time. For example, you might be used to checking your cell phone while eating, or you might have a habit of texting while walking. Although it may seem very efficient to do multiple things at once, in reality, such multitasking usually doesn't help people be more productive. Instead, it mostly just adds to their stress. Informal mindfulness is all about doing just one thing at a time, with full awareness.

Try This! Mindfully STOPping and Informal Mindfulness

Here are some examples of daily activities that can become mindfulness practices:

- Brushing your teeth

- Walking to class

- Getting dressed in the morning

- Walking your dog or petting your cat

- Cleaning your room

- Answering your phone

- Exercising or playing sports

- Playing a musical instrument

- Drawing or painting

Can you think of some more?

Pick at least one of these activities as a means of practicing informal mindfulness over the coming week.

The first step, before doing this activity, is the mindful STOP practice (adapted with permission from Stahl and Goldstein 2010):

STOP

S: Stop whatever you are doing. If you were about to start a new activity, just pause for a moment instead.

T: Take three mindful breaths.

O: Observe what is happening around you in the present moment. Check in with yourself as well: What is happening inside of you right now?

P: Proceed mindfully with whatever it was you were doing or were about to do.

After mindfully STOPping, proceed with the activity as if it is the most important thing in the world, with great curiosity and care. As you do the activity, tune in to your senses. What does this thing that you are doing look like? What does it smell like? What does it sound like? What does it feel like?

You don't need to rush to get whatever it is you're doing done. You don't need to do three things at once. Let go of all that extra stress. Doing just this one thing, with mindfulness, is enough. If you are walking, just walk. If you are eating, just eat. If you are brushing your teeth, just brush—instead of trying to get it done quickly so that you can move on to something else, invest 100 percent of your effort in brushing your teeth.

As best you can, keep your full attention on what you are doing. Continue to breathe mindfully. Every time your mind wanders, simply notice: *Where did my mind just go?* Whenever stress arises—for example, when you start to think about all the things that you need to do or wish you had done—just come back to your breath. Don't judge yourself if your mind is wandering; you're not doing anything wrong. Remember, noticing that your mind wandered marks a moment of mindfulness. STOP, taking three more breaths. Return to the present moment, over and over again.

You can say a few guiding words silently to yourself to help you stay present. For example, if you are walking to class or to the bus stop, you can say to yourself, *Breathing in, I know that I am walking. Breathing out, I smile. Walking… Smiling…*

How is this experience different from your normal way of doing things? Do you notice anything interesting about this daily activity that you might not have noticed before? How might paying attention to everyday activities in this way help you be less stressed and more resilient?

Bells of Mindfulness

In sitting meditation, people sometimes use the sound of a bell to bring their attention to their own sitting. At Plum Village, we learned to use any type of bell sound we heard during our day as a cue to be mindful. Every time we heard the phone ring or a church bell ringing in the distance, we would stop talking, stop walking, and come back to the present moment. After three mindful breaths, we would continue whatever we were doing, but more mindfully. This is a practice that I have continued to this day.

Try This! Bells of Mindfulness

What are some things that you see or hear in your daily life that you might use as "bells of mindfulness"? A bell of mindfulness could be a real bell that you hear, or it could be some other sound or sight in your environment that can remind you to shift out of autopilot and wake up to the present moment. Here are some examples:

- A cell phone ringing

- A bird singing

- The sound of laughter

- A stop sign on the road

Can you think of any more?

The next time you hear or see one of these "bells," take it as an invitation to STOP, shift out of autopilot, and practice informal mindfulness. Stop what you were doing (if it is safe to do so). Take three mindful breaths, coming fully to the present moment. Then, continue what you were doing, as mindfully as you can. Notice whether doing this changes your experience in any way.

Mindful Eating: Making Life More Delicious

You probably eat several times a day. But how often are you truly present for the experience of eating? How often do you really taste the food, savor the flavors, and appreciate where the food has come from? If you're like me, you have a tendency to eat on autopilot—as quickly as possible while on your computer or phone or busy worrying about the day. Any time you eat like this, mealtime becomes just another time to stress.

Eating a meal mindfully can be a wonderful meditation practice, as well as a break from the stress of the day. When you eat with curiosity and beginner's mind, you can really savor each bite. You can just eat your food with 100 percent of your attention, instead of chewing on your worries and stress of the day. You might suddenly discover how interesting and enjoyable your meal can be. Experiment with mindful eating (also called eating meditation) the next time you sit down for a meal.

Try This! Mindful Eating

First, stop whatever else you are doing, so that you can be fully present with just eating. Turn off your cell phone and other electronic devices. Breathe in and out three times. You might wish to reflect on the food in front of you, aware of and grateful for the natural source of the food and the work of the many people who made your meal possible.

Once you are fully present, begin eating. Eat with curiosity and beginner's mind, just as you practiced with the raisin (in chapter 2). Bring your full awareness to each bite, chewing slowly. Take your time—there's no need to rush. Notice the small details of the tastes and textures, as well as the sensations of chewing and swallowing. Notice also what is happening in your mind as you eat. Every time you notice your mind is wandering, tune back in to your mindful breathing. When you are fully present again, continue eating, as mindfully as you can. When you are finished with your meal, breathe in and out mindfully three times, and thank yourself for having taken care of yourself through mindful eating.

If you wish to make mindful eating a regular practice, it is often easiest when there are no other people or distractions. For example, if you eat breakfast alone at home every day, see whether you can transform that routine into "eating breakfast meditation" every day for the next week. Once you are comfortable with this practice, you may wish to invite your friends or family to join you in mindful eating.

What do you notice when doing this practice? How does eating mindfully change your experience of eating?

✻ *Margaret's Story*

Margaret had been skeptical about some of the informal mindfulness practices we tried in the mindfulness course, especially eating meditation. She admitted, "I hated doing eating meditation at first. I felt like people were staring at me. It just made me more stressed out."

She had decided to keep practicing, even though it felt weird at first. By the end of the course, she declared, "Now I'm doing eating meditation on my own all the time. It's nice. For example, I drink coffee in the morning. Now, I really notice what I'm drinking, instead of just drinking just to stay awake. It tastes so much better that way, and my day is better when I start my morning with mindfulness."

Three Minutes of Freedom from Stress: The SOBER Breathing Space

There will no doubt be occasions throughout your day when you have a few minutes of "time to kill." Let's say you are standing at the bus stop, waiting for the bus. Or perhaps you are sitting in the car or on the bus, on your way to school or to your friend's house. These brief interludes are wonderful opportunities for you to engage in a short mindfulness practice called the SOBER Breathing Space (adapted with permission from Bowen, Chawla, and Marlatt 2011).

As you might have guessed from the name, the SOBER Breathing Space was originally developed to help people who are recovering from alcohol or drug addiction. The SOBER practice is a link between formal and informal mindfulness practice. Use it to intentionally shift out of autopilot and bring mindful awareness into whatever situation you find yourself in.

Try This! The SOBER Breathing Space

You can do this mindfulness practice using the instructions below or with the help of the recording (track 6) available at http://www.newharbinger.com/30802.

Picture an hourglass—wide at the top, narrow in the middle, and wide again at the bottom. Your field of awareness over the course of the SOBER practice will follow that shape: wide at the beginning and end of the practice, narrow and focused in the middle.

You can practice the SOBER Breathing Space while standing, while sitting, or while lying down. You can practice it with your eyes open or closed. You can practice it inside or outside, in a quiet place or a noisy one. Try it once a day for the next seven days, and see whether it changes your day and your experience of stress. Simply follow the steps below. The acronym SOBER makes them easy to remember.

1. **Stop.** Stop whatever you are doing. If you were about to start a new activity, pause for a moment instead. Shift out of autopilot, and enter deeply into the present moment.

2. **Observe.** Simply observe what is happening, with beginner's mind and self-compassion. What is happening right now, inside your body? What emotions are arising in you right now? What thoughts are coming up in this moment? You don't need to change, "fix," or judge anything—just observe.

3. **Breathe.** This is the narrow part of the hourglass. For the next minute or so, invite your awareness to rest on only your breath. Just ride the waves of your breath. You can say quietly to yourself, *Breathing in, I know that I am breathing in. Breathing out, I know that I am breathing out. In… Out…* Every time your mind wanders, simply notice that: *Hello, wandering mind!* Then, gently bring your

awareness back to your breath. You may need to do this repeatedly, and that's okay.

4. **Expand.** This is the wide part of the hourglass at the bottom. Continue to breathe, and expand your awareness back to a sensation
of breathing with your whole body. Check in again with what is happening in your body—are there any sensations? Is there any pain?
Check in again with your emotions—what feelings are present for
you right now? Check in again with your thoughts—what thoughts
are arising in your mind right now? Is this moment any different than
when you started the practice?

5. **Respond.** Respond mindfully to the situation. Instead of automatically doing whatever you usually would in this situation, see what
new choices and possibilities may have opened up. Approach the
situation as an informal mindfulness practice, bringing the mindful
spirit in as best you can.

―――――――――――**Teen Voices:** *Nicole T.*―――――――

"I use the SOBER Breathing Space a lot, just to come back to
the present moment and stop ruminating. The breathing space
kind of takes my focus away from all of my stress, and I can just
focus on one thing. It's really calming just to be able to stop and
breathe for a few minutes, because we're always so busy, we're
always so stressed—just having two minutes or three minutes to
breathe is really helpful."

Mindful living can be a beautiful art, and I am sure you can become a talented artist. With the energy of mindfulness, you can touch the present moment deeply throughout the day, and you can protect yourself from stress. The more you are there for your mindfulness practice, the more your mindfulness practice will be there for you during times of stress. Practice mindfulness in small ways throughout your day and see what happens to your stress levels.

Chapter 8

Mindfulness in Motion

When I dance, I dance; when I sleep, I sleep...and when I walk
alone in a beautiful orchard, if my thoughts drift to far-off
matters for some part of the time, for some other part I lead
them back again to the walk, the orchard, to the sweetness of
this solitude, to myself.

— sixteenth-century essayist
Michel de Montaigne

Contrary to popular belief, meditation isn't always about
sitting still. And it's not just about using your mind.
Mindfulness is an *embodied* practice, meaning one in which
you use your whole mind, heart, and body. Yoga masters,
practitioners of tai chi, dancers, and many others have known
for a long time that movement can relieve stress. The healing
power in all yoga and "internal" martial arts (such as tai chi)
lies in deep awareness of the body.

Mindful Walking

You walk all the time—for example, to and from school or the bus stop and from class to class. But, how often are you truly present with each step as you walk? Perhaps most of the time you are lost in thought, thinking about where you are going instead of where you are at that moment. And by the time you get there, maybe you're already thinking about the next place you will go or the next thing you will do. You put a destination in front of you and chase after it, never truly arriving.

Walking meditation is a radically different way of walking. It involves shifting out of autopilot and walking just for the sake of walking. Rather than focus on where you are trying to go, you bring your awareness to the act of walking itself. You don't even need to have a destination—you can walk in circles if you want to. When you walk mindfully, you arrive in the present moment with every step, becoming deeply in touch with life in the here and now. Your path becomes a mindful journey. Your steps are in harmony with your breath, and your body begins to feel more relaxed and at ease.

Walking meditation is one of my favorite practices. In the morning, I tend to get anxious and stressed about all the things that I need to do that day. So I practice walking meditation every morning on my way to work. Every time I start mentally going over my to-do list, I remind myself to come back to the present moment. I remember to breathe, and I bring my full awareness to my next step. Instead of continuing to stress, I bring my full awareness to the simple act of walking. I also look up and enjoy the sight of the flowers on the bushes as I walk past and the sound of the birds singing overhead. When I walk in this way, my mornings are much more enjoyable and less stressful.

Walking meditation can be a formal meditation or an informal one. In formal walking meditation, you walk slowly and with great care, not going anywhere in particular. With informal walking meditation, you practice any time you walk anywhere, such as when you walk to school, to the bus stop, or from one room of your house to another. With each step, you will strengthen your mindfulness muscle and find more mental balance, freedom, and resilience. Each step will nourish your mindfulness and resilience, helping you let go of stress.

Try This! Walking Meditation

You can do formal walking meditation using the instructions below or with the help of the recording (track 6) available at http://www.newharbinger .com/30802.

Formal Walking Meditation

For this practice, you can walk around in a circle in your living room or another room of your house. You can also try walking around your yard, around the block, on a nearby trail, or in a park.

Before you start walking, stand tall like a mountain. Breathe mindfully in and out three times, establishing yourself 100 percent in the present moment. Breathing in mindfully, take one step. Breathing out mindfully, take the next step. Walk slowly, continuing to synchronize your breath with your steps. Notice how your feet feel as they touch the ground. Notice how it feels for your body to be in motion and moving through your environment. If this practice feels awkward or weird, just notice that too. Every time your mind wanders, or every time stress arises, simply breathe and smile. Bring your complete attention back to the next step, the next breath, arriving again in the present moment.

You can silently recite a simple verse as you walk, to help yourself stay present. Say one phrase silently with each step and each breath: *I have arrived. I am home. In the here. In the now. Arrived… Home… Here… Now…*

Informal Walking Meditation

Practice walking mindfully as you go to school, whenever you go up or down a flight of stairs, as you walk to the bus stop, or as you walk around your house. You'll probably need to walk more quickly than you would during formal walking meditation, but you can still do it with the same mindful awareness. Continue to synchronize your breath with your steps, experimenting with the rhythm. You may find that your in-breath is naturally a bit shorter than your out-breath. For example, you might take two steps with each in-breath and three steps with each out-breath.

Instead of getting lost in thought as you walk, intentionally notice your surroundings. Notice the fresh air, the sunshine, the people, the plants, or the animals. Appreciate the wonders of life that you might take for granted if you were in autopilot mode.

Daily Walking Meditation

Practice walking meditation for a few minutes every day this week. Experiment with this practice in the spirit of beginner's mind, as if you were relearning how to walk. Start with slow, formal walking meditation. Then, experiment with informal walking meditation as you go about your daily life. Go on a mindful hike on the beach or through a park. Practice walking meditation when you are feeling stressed, perhaps imagining that you are letting go of a little bit of stress every time you put your front foot down onto the ground. See what you can discover about your steps, your breath, and your inner resilience.

Teen Voices: *Nicole T.*

"I've done some mindful walking, just today—walking to school. It was the first day back at school. I was really nervous, and I didn't really want to see certain people. So to just get back into the present moment, I was walking, so I just walked more mindfully and paid attention to the muscles in my feet and what I was doing. It helped me stop worrying about it... I was doing mindful walking when I was going to my classes. No one really notices if you're just paying attention to your feet. So I was able to do that [on my way] to my classes, and it was really, really helpful. It really helped me stay calm. I was able to concentrate a lot more in class, and I didn't fall asleep, which was good!"

Mindful Movement

Mindful movement is a practice of moving your body slowly, intentionally, with deep care and attention to what is happening in the present moment. It is a lot like yoga or tai chi, except that your specific postures or movements don't matter that much. You're not necessarily "exercising" or trying to get a stretch or a workout. You're not competing with anyone, even yourself. In this practice, exactly what you do

103

with your body doesn't really matter. What's most important is to simply be fully present with your body, with your movements, and with your breath.

Try This! Mindful Movement

You can do this mindfulness practice using the instructions below or with the help of the recording (track 7) available at http://www.newharbinger.com/30802.

This is only an example of a sequence of movements that you can practice. If you already know a yoga or stretching routine, you can do that instead. You can even make up your own movements. What matters is that you bring mindful awareness to your body and move gently as you breathe in and out, honoring your intention to be present.

As you go through each movement, pay attention to the messages and sensations that arise in your body. Any time you notice stress or tension, bring special attention to that part of your body. Breathe deeply in and out through that part of your body, seeing whether that allows your body to release some stress or tension.

Caution: During mindful movement, it is important to listen to your body, especially if you have any health issues or injuries. If a particular movement causes you pain, do not force yourself to do it. Modify the movement so that it works for your body, or skip it entirely and just practice mindful standing or sitting instead.

1. **Stand like a mountain.** Stand with your feet about shoulder-width apart. Keep your knees slightly bent, and allow your shoulders to drop slightly. Lift the top of your head toward the sky. Notice what

this feels like. Breathe mindfully three times, taking deeper breaths than you might naturally take.

2. **Roll your shoulders.** With the next breath in, in a slow, gentle motion, lift your shoulders up toward your ears. With the next breath out, slowly and gently roll your shoulders backward and down. Repeat, rolling your shoulders in sync with your breath, four times. Notice what your shoulders feel like.

3. **Roll your neck.** With the next breath out, gently bring your chin down toward your chest, so that you are looking at the ground. With the next breath in, gently roll your neck to one side, bringing your ear toward your shoulder. With the next breath out, roll your neck back to center, looking down again. With the next breath in, roll your neck to the other side. Repeat, rolling your neck in sync with your breath, four times. Take a moment to check in—how does your neck feel right now? Are there any areas of tightness or tension, or does it feel loose and relaxed?

4. **Stretch your arms.** Breathing in, bring your arms straight out from your sides, palms up, all the way up over your head. Breathing out, slowly lower your arms, palms facing down, in front of your chest and abdomen and then down to your sides. Repeat, making slow, gentle circles with your arms, in sync with your breath, four times. Allow the deep, cleansing breaths to wash through your body.

5. **Hang like a rag doll.** With the next breath out, bend forward. Instead of curving your back, try to allow your spine to lengthen just a tiny bit and bend at the waist. Bend your knees slightly. Allow your arms to dangle loosely. Maintaining this position, just breathe mindfully in and out five times, noticing what this position feels like for your body.

6. **Sit and bend forward.** Take a seat on the floor or on a chair, with your feet in front of you. With the next breath out, reach your hands out in front of you, toward your feet. If you are sitting on the floor, you can bend your knees slightly, if that's more comfortable. Again, allow your spine to lengthen just a tiny bit. Maintaining this gentle stretch, just breathe deeply in and out five times, noticing your breath and the sensations in your body.

7. **Twist.** Remain seated. With the next breath out, place your right hand on your left hip. Place your left hand behind your back, reaching toward your right hip. Look over your left shoulder. Breathe in and out. Try to lengthen your spine a little bit, sitting as tall as you can. Continue to breathe like this four more times. On the fifth breath out, come back to center. Breathe in deeply. Breathe out, twisting to the other side, and hold for five more mindful breaths.

Experiment with practicing mindful movement just before you practice sitting meditation or the body scan. Or, practice one or two brief mindful movements any time your body feels stiff or tense—for example, after you have been sitting for a long time at your desk. Let go of any mental stress as you come back to your body.

Practice mindful walking and mindful movement with the same care and attention that you would give to sitting meditation or the body scan. If sitting or lying still is very difficult for you, you may particularly enjoy these "moving meditations." Whether you are sitting or standing, moving or not moving, you can practice mindfulness to let go of stress any time and anywhere.

Chapter 9

Seeing Your Thoughts As Only Thoughts

We are but a product of our thoughts.
What we think, we become.

— twentieth-century civil rights leader
Mahatma Gandhi

In the quote above, Gandhi observed how powerful thoughts can be—how your thoughts can become your reality. If you constantly have stressful, depressing, or anxiety-producing thoughts, then your mood and your entire reality will become stressed, depressed, or anxious. The good news is you are more than your thoughts. Thoughts are like clouds or weather in the sky. Even as the storm clouds come through and the rain pours down, the great clear blue sky is still there overhead. It hasn't gone anywhere, even though it may not be easy to see in that moment, hidden behind the clouds.

Your own mind is like that, too. Even when negative thoughts are storming in your mind, you still have your mindfulness and your conscious breathing that you can get back in touch with. There are still positive elements in your life (like your pet kitten cuddling with you, or the beautiful flowers that are growing outside your window) that you can be grateful for, if you can remember to see them with awareness. Breathing mindfully through the storms of negative thinking allows your clear and spacious mind to reemerge from behind the clouds. In other words, even though you may have negative thoughts, you don't have to be trapped in them. You can tap into the wisdom and resilience that lives in your breath and in your body, anytime and anywhere. With mindfulness, you have the power to free yourself from upsetting thoughts by coming back to the present moment.

Teen Voices: *Jaclyn*

"I was getting bad anxiety about English class. I was hyperventilating before class. I was overthinking. [So] I tried meditating every day before class. Over a few days, [my anxiety] got better. I wasn't thinking so much about why I didn't want to be there.

"I feel like my anxiety is unrealistic. I think about things that are unrealistic. Mindfulness helps me get back to the real world."

My friend and colleague Jake Locke developed the following exercise (inspired by Isabel Hargreaves; see Segal, Williams, and Teasdale 2013) for the mindfulness course for teens at our hospital (personal communication, September 10, 2014). In this exercise, you'll witness the powerful influence that your mood has on your thoughts.

Exercise: In the School Cafeteria

Imagine the following scenario. As you do, observe what thoughts and images arise in your mind.

Scenario 1. It's lunchtime, and you're on your way to the school cafeteria. You're in a bad mood, because your teacher just criticized you in front of the class for a project that you had done. You're feeling stressed. (Take a moment to imagine how that stress would feel for you, emotionally and in your body.) In the cafeteria, you notice one of your friends among the crowd. You wave to her, but she doesn't wave back.

What would you think? What kinds of thoughts and explanations are coming up for you about why your friend didn't wave back?

Now imagine the following slightly different scenario. As you do, observe what thoughts and images arise in your mind.

Scenario 2. It's lunchtime, and you're on your way to the school cafeteria. You're in a good mood, because your teacher just praised you for a project that you had done. You're feeling really happy. (Take a moment to imagine how that happiness would feel for you, emotionally and in your body.) In the cafeteria, you notice one of your friends among the crowd. You wave to her, but she doesn't wave back.

What would you think? Are your thoughts about what might be going on in this scenario any different than for the first scenario?

Thoughts Are Just Thoughts

When teens imagine the first scenario in the "School Cafeteria" exercise, they often notice thoughts like *She must have been mad at me* or *Maybe she was talking about me behind my back*. Their thoughts about this scenario are often negative and self-critical. When imagining the second scenario, they usually report thinking something like *She must have been too busy, Maybe she's having a bad day*, or *I wouldn't take it personally*. Often, their thoughts about this scenario are much less negative and more empathetic and understanding. Was this true for you?

The only real difference between the two scenarios is your mood. In both scenarios, you have very limited information about why your friend didn't wave back to you. Yet, you make some important assumptions. Any time you are in a bad mood, you are more likely to make negative assumptions. The lesson is that the thoughts you have about any given situation are not necessarily facts. If thoughts were always true, your mood could not possibly have any bearing on your interpretation of a situation.

Let's continue to explore the connection between your mood and your way of thinking.

Try This! Common Automatic Thoughts

Some people report that they frequently experience certain negative thoughts. For them, these negative thoughts come up automatically in many different situations. On a separate piece of paper (or just in your head), rate each of the following such thoughts (adapted with permission from Hollon and Kendall 1980) on a scale of 1 to 5 according to how much you believe that thought yourself, where 1 is "not at all" and 5 is "completely." (If you're feeling really stressed out, depressed, or anxious right now, skip this exercise for the time being and come back to it later.)

1. I am useless.

2. Nothing ever works out for me.

3. I fail at everything.

4. I just shouldn't exist.

5. No one likes me.

6. I'm a loser.

7. People don't understand me.

8. There is nothing to look forward to.

9. I wish I could change my life.

10. I'm a really bad person.

11. I will always feel miserable.

12. I disappoint everyone.

13. My life is a disaster.

14. Everyone hates me.

15. What's the point?

16. I'm stupid.

17. *I will never be good enough.*

18. *I can't stand myself.*

19. *I'm a burden on all those around me.*

20. *No one would ever want to know the real me.*

Now, imagine that you're feeling really stressed out, depressed, or anxious. Take another look at the list. Can you see how your ratings might change as a result of feeling this way?

At times when you are feeling good, you are not as likely to believe the type of thoughts listed in the preceding exercise, so they may not come up. However, at times when you are feeling stressed or depressed, these thoughts may pop up in your mind more frequently, and you may be more likely to believe them. Not only does your mood affect your way of thinking, but your way of thinking affects your mood. For example, just reading a list of negative thoughts—as in the preceding exercise—can make some people feel a little sad.

Here's the bottom line: thoughts are just thoughts—thoughts are not facts. Don't believe everything you think!

Rumination and Stress

Cows, sheep, deer, and camels all belong to a group of mammals called *ruminants*. Have you ever watched a cow chewing grass? The cow chews the same mouthful over and over, and over again. That's what "rumination" means: to chew repeatedly, for an extended time. Just like a cow chewing on its cud, you may sometimes ruminate on your own negative thoughts. Whenever you get stressed out, you may end up thinking over and over about your problem. For example, if you're having a hard time while taking a test, you might keep thinking, *I should have studied more; I'm going to fail;* and *What's wrong with me?* Rumination can be like watching the same scene from a movie over and over again in your mind.

Sometimes, a negative thought can quickly lead to another negative thought, and then to a whole train of negative thoughts. For example, *I'm going to fail this exam* leads to *I'm going to fail this class* leads to *I'm never going to get accepted into college*—and it doesn't stop there. Before you know it, your mind has created a story and taken you on a "runaway train," leading to doubts and worries about your entire life!

Rumination also activates your lizard brain, distorting your way of thinking and your perceptions even further. As discussed in chapter 1, you have the same fight, flight, or freeze reaction whether you are facing a real tiger or a paper tiger of your mind's creation. Your own distorted thoughts activate your body's stress response and your lizard brain, and your lizard brain distorts your thoughts even further. You can end up in a downward spiral of stress and rumination.

Trying to "think your way out of a problem" is a type of rumination that is sometimes oddly irresistible. You might feel as though if you just keep thinking and thinking about the problem, you'll eventually find a solution. Unfortunately, that rarely works, and it usually just makes you more stressed. People who often ruminate may also tend to develop

113

unhealthy coping behaviors—like getting drunk or getting high, or Internet or video game addictions—in an attempt to quiet their minds and escape from difficult thoughts. The problem is that you can never truly escape from your own mind, and attempts to do so usually cause more stress. So what is the healthy alternative?

Not Getting on the Train

Whenever you are stressed out, it's easy for you to get stuck "in your head." Any time you can "get out of your head" by bringing your full awareness to your breath or to your body, you can temporarily free yourself from rumination or other repetitive thoughts. Sometimes, even just a short break from rumination can be enough for you to regain your mental balance and respond more skillfully to a difficult situation.

Meditating can also help. *How can I possibly meditate when my mind is going round and round?* you may be wondering. If so, let me assure you that meditating doesn't mean "getting rid of thinking" or having an "empty mind." It does, however, involve mindfulness of thoughts—paying attention to your thoughts as they arise, moment to moment. When you meditate, you observe your thoughts with kindness and curiosity, neither holding on to nor pushing away any particular thoughts. This gives you an opportunity to learn about the nature of your own thinking and observe how thinking and stress are related. Freeing yourself from unnecessary stress doesn't in the least involve changing or controlling your thoughts. Instead, it involves changing the nature of your relationship with them.

One way to understand this is if rumination is like getting carried away by a stressful train of thought, mindfulness of thoughts can help you keep your feet on the ground and free you from those stressful thoughts (Biegel 2009). Imagine that you are standing on a hill above the tracks, watching your train of thought go by. Each thought is a train car. The next car (the next thought) might be the same as the one before it, or it might be different. Instead of jumping on any particular thought and riding the train, you can remain firmly planted, just observing, until all the cars pass out of view. By not getting on that train, you let go of unnecessary stress caused by rumination.

Another way to approach mindfulness of thoughts is to imagine that you are watching your thoughts pass by like clouds. In this scenario, the sky represents your mind. Sometimes there are no clouds, and your mind is clear and spacious. Other times, there are lots of clouds, floating past very quickly. Just as in life, you can't keep clouds from coming, nor can you make them stay. You can only watch as they come and go. By just watching your thoughts instead of trying to control them, you will become more at peace with your own mind.

Or you can imagine that you are sitting at the edge of a stream, and each thought that arises is a leaf being carried along with the current (Hayes, Strosahl, and Wilson 1999). You are watching the leaves float by. Whenever you find yourself walking downstream because you are being "pulled" by a particular leaf, you can make a mindful choice to let it go, sit back down, and continue watching the leaves floating past. Again, the purpose of the practice is to help you avoid getting carried away by stressful thoughts, by coming back to present-moment awareness.

Try This! Mindfulness of Thinking

You can do this mindfulness practice using the instructions below or with the help of the recording (track 8) available at http://www.newharbinger.com/30802.

Try this meditation for three to five minutes. You can do it while sitting or lying down.

First, practice mindfully STOPping. Stop whatever it is you are doing. Breathe mindfully three times, coming back to the present moment.

Next, observe your thoughts using one of the modes of imagery discussed— imagine your thoughts as train cars, clouds in the sky, or leaves on a stream. Whichever mode you choose, simply observe your thoughts as they come into view and for however long they stay in the picture. Notice whether you're having lots of thoughts, fast thoughts, or slow thoughts. Observe your thoughts with kindness and curiosity, without getting caught up in them. If no thoughts are arising in your mind, simply notice that.

Experiment with silently labeling each thought using one word, according to category, such as "planning," "worrying," "memory," or "rumination."

You don't need to try to figure out whether your thoughts are true or not. You don't need to suppress certain thoughts or judge yourself for having them. And you don't need to get carried away by the story your mind creates. Every time you feel lost, confused, or overwhelmed, remember that mindful breathing is always there for you. Simply come back to the next breath, and return to the present moment. When you're ready, bring your attention back to your thinking, and observe what thoughts are arising now. You can go back and forth in this way as many times as you need to.

Lizard-brain thinking and rumination can add to your stress. But you are more than your thoughts. Even when your mind is filled with stressful thoughts, you can still tap into your inner clarity, strength, and resilience. With mindfulness, you can recognize when your lizard brain is activated. Instead of fighting it, you can say hello (and good-bye) to rumination when it arises. *Hello, lizard brain! Hello, rumination! I recognize you. I know that you're just trying to keep me safe. Thanks, but I'm okay—I don't really need you right now.* Then, with a gentle smile, you can breathe mindfully and come back to reality in the present moment.

✳ Part 2 ✳

Applying Mindfulness: Handling Stressful Situations

Chapter 10

The Art of Stress: Handling Difficult Emotions

When [difficult] feelings arise, you have to practice in order
to use the energy of mindfulness to recognize them, embrace
them, look deeply into them. It's like a mother when the baby
is crying. Your anxiety is your baby. You have to take care of
it. You have to go back to yourself, recognize the suffering in
you, embrace the suffering, and you get relief.

— Zen Master, poet, activist, and
Nobel Peace Prize nominee
Thich Nhat Hanh (2010)

Stress often leads to depression, anxiety, or anger. Depression,
anxiety, or anger can quickly become overwhelming, getting
in the way of living your life—perhaps even causing you to
do things that hurt yourself or other people. Still, although
such emotions can be uncomfortable and difficult, there are

no "bad" emotions. In keeping with the quote above, you can think of your emotions as children. Just as there are no "bad" children, all emotions deserve to be treated with kindness and compassion. When you can stay with and even embrace difficult emotions with mindfulness, you will experience an incredible sense of freedom. You will no longer fear difficult emotions, because you will know that you have the power to handle them.

✳ *Joseph's Story*

Joseph, a college freshman, suffered from chronic stress and anxiety, mostly related to school. In our second mindfulness session together, he shared how he had been able to use guided meditation to handle stress since our first session: "I was feeling really stressed and panicky all day long. Sitting in class, trying to do my homework later—every time I felt panicky, I put on my headphones and listened to a guided meditation. It helped me chill out, stay in class, and get through my day."

Don't Just Do Something, Sit There!

When you are feeling a strong emotion like anger, depression, or anxiety, that is a signal that your stress response is activated. Your lizard brain is interpreting everything as a threat and is trying to help you survive by fighting back or running away.

In that moment, you might feel as if you have to do something right away: *Don't just sit there, do something!* your lizard brain urges. But when your lizard brain is activated, acting on that emotion is likely to make the situation worse, not better. Handling that moment with mindfulness means flipping the script. As Thich Nhat Hanh often says, "Don't just do something, sit there!" Stop whatever it is that you were about to say or do, shift out of autopilot, and take a moment to just be aware of your emotion instead of acting on it (see "Mindfully STOPping and Informal Mindfulness" in chapter 7). In this way, you can tame your lizard brain and reengage your human brain. You will see the situation more clearly and be able to handle it more wisely.

You Can't Fight the Waves, but You Can Learn to Surf

When you're experiencing a strong emotion, it might seem as if it will last forever. You might think, *I'm so anxious right now I can't stand it*, or *I'm always going to feel depressed.* But emotions come and go, like waves in the ocean. We often try so hard to avoid strong emotions. But trying to run away from your emotions is exhausting and usually causes more stress. It's like trying to fight the waves in the ocean. You might find a moment when you think you've escaped, but then you get knocked over by the next wave.

Jon Kabat-Zinn points out, "You can't stop the waves, but you can learn to surf" (1994, 29). Instead of trying to fight the waves of emotions, you can learn to ride those waves with mindfulness, skill, and compassion. Like a surfer on the ocean, you may experience some light waves, and some very intense ones. Some may even knock you down. But you can always get back up. Your "surfboard" is your mindful breathing, and it is always there for you. So, don't try to push the waves away. Don't try to hold on to them. Remember that whatever emotion you are experiencing won't last forever. Know that just as you are more than your pain (see chapter 6) and more than your thoughts (see chapter 9), you are more than your difficult emotion in that moment. Even when things are difficult, you still have wisdom and resilience inside of you that can help you survive any wave. So just stay present, continue to breathe, and ride the waves as they come and go.

Getting Out of Your Head

Any time you are anxious, depressed, or angry about something, you can easily get stuck "in your head" and lost in rumination, thinking about what made you upset and how bad you feel. Unfortunately, this usually just increases your stress.

Emotions affect not only your mind, but also your body. Think of common expressions like "I was so scared I pooped my pants," "My heart is broken," and "That made me feel sick to my stomach." Where do your own emotions tend to have effects in your body? When you are angry, worried, or sad, how do you experience that in your body?

When you're experiencing a strong emotion, the safest way to be with it is to get out of your head and focus on how you experience the emotion *in your body*. By becoming intimately aware of your breath and your body sensations, you can make wise use of the signals coming from your body.

The SOBER Breathing Space that you learned in chapter 7 can be great for handling difficult emotions like anger, worry, and sadness. The SOBER practice isn't meant as an escape or a fix for difficult emotions. What the SOBER practice does is help you get out of your head and into your body, stepping out of the vicious cycle of rumination. This helps you avoid automatically reacting in lizard-brain mode and shift into mindful awareness. Your mindfulness can then open you up to new possibilities, and perhaps a more creative and compassionate response to a difficult situation.

Try This! The SOBER Coping Space

You can do this mindfulness practice (adapted with permission from Bowen, Chawla, and Marlatt 2011) using the instructions below or with the help of the recording (track 9) available at http://www.newharbinger.com/30802.

In this exercise, you will intentionally bring to mind a difficult situation, and then practice the SOBER Breathing Space (chapter 7) to help you handle any difficult emotion that arises as a result.

Invite to mind some difficulty that's happening in your life right now, one that isn't too intense or overwhelming. For example, you may wish to think of a recent stressful homework assignment or a minor argument that you had with a friend. Once you have something in mind, notice what difficult emotion(s) is associated with this difficulty for you. Then, begin the SOBER practice:

1. **Stop.** Any time you are experiencing a difficult emotion, the first step to handling it is simply to recognize what is happening. For example, recognize *I'm stressed right now*, or *I'm upset*. Instead of reacting automatically out of frustration or anger, just stop what you are doing, or wait before doing whatever you were about to do.

2. **Observe.** What is going on inside of you right now?

   Check in with your body, just as it is, right now. How are you experiencing this emotion in your body and in your breath? Is there tightness in your chest? Is there a knot in your stomach? Is your breath rapid and shallow? Get to know your emotions through the window of your body. Trust the wisdom of your body, because it is telling you something that is worth listening to. Those sensations are your body's way of telling you that you need some care and attention because you are stressed. Listen to your body with compassion, allowing yourself to experience whatever is happening within you.

   Check in with your emotion. Recognize the emotion by its name, and offer it a friendly greeting. For example, *Hello, sadness. I recognize you. I'm going to take care of you*. It's okay to feel whatever it is you are feeling. As best you can, allow it to be, just as it is.

   Check in with your thinking. Are you trying to think your way out of this problem? Are you ruminating? If you are, simply notice that. Then, make a mindful choice to "not get on the train" and instead just ride the waves of your breath.

3. **Breathe.** For the next minute or so, allow your awareness to rest only on your breath. Every time your mind wanders to thoughts about your difficulty, bring your awareness back to your breath. *In... Out... In... Out...* If you need to think about anything at all, just think about your breath.

4. **Expand.** Expand your awareness.

    Notice what sensations are present in your body right now. Invite them into your awareness.

    Observe what emotions are present right now. If calmness is present, notice that. If difficult emotions are still present, that's okay too. Reoognize that you are more than your difficult emotions. Your difficult emotions are present, and now your mindfulness is also present, to help you take care of those emotions.

    Check in with your thoughts again. Where are they now? Are you still ruminating?

5. **Respond.** Respond mindfully to the situation.

    This time, because you are only imagining a difficult situation, simply end the exercise and see whether you can carry on with your day more mindfully. In the future, if you are practicing the SOBER Coping Space in response to a real-life difficult situation, see whether it has opened up some flexibility for you as you reenter the situation mindfully. Are you aware of new ways you might respond to the difficult situation? Do you have more clarity, more calmness in you, to handle the situation wisely and compassionately? Can you resume what you were doing—for example, can you get back to your homework, or finish taking your test, or talk to the person who stressed you out—infused with the mindful spirit?

    If you are still feeling an intense emotion—if your lizard brain is still activated—you might instead choose to take a longer break from the situation. A wise response in that case might be to practice sitting meditation or go do something else that is nourishing or enjoyable. If you make this choice, it doesn't mean that the SOBER practice didn't work. In fact, it shows that you have enough awareness and self-compassion to make a mindful choice in a difficult situation. The most important thing is to take good care of yourself and to shift out of lizard-brain mode before trying to solve the problem.

Experiment with this practice the next time you're under stress and experiencing a difficult emotion, like anger, fear, depression, or worry. See whether the SOBER Coping Space helps you handle the emotion and respond to the situation more mindfully.

Move, Breathe, and Embrace Your Difficult Emotions

Sometimes, the wisest thing to do first when you are really upset is move your body. It might be just too hard to sit still when you're extremely upset, because your body is in fight, flight, or freeze mode. Instead of trying to force yourself to sit still, you can get out of your head and into your body. Vigorous movement and exercise can help you burn up excess adrenaline, helping your body move through (and out of) fight, flight, or freeze mode.

After moving your body, you can practice mindful belly breathing, in a practice that is inspired by Thich Nhat Hanh (2007, 189–90; 2009, 86–91) and Mother Nature. In this practice, you imagine that you are a tree in the midst of an intense storm. To survive the storm, you keep your primary attention on the strongest part of you, which is your trunk, or your belly. The practices of moving and belly breathing can help you regain the stability and strength that you need to take care of the difficult emotion.

Once you are stable and clear enough, you can embrace and soothe your difficult emotion with mindfulness. In chapter 6, you learned that *Suffering = Pain x Resistance.* You learned that you can handle pain in your body by letting go of resistance to pain and accepting the sensation just as it is, moment-to-moment. You can handle painful emotions the same way. Mindfulness and self-compassion can help you stop fighting, and stop running away from, difficult emotions. You can simply allow difficult emotions to be, just as they are. You can even turn toward your difficult emotions, holding those feelings with gentle care and awareness. In this way, you can befriend and make peace with your emotions and with yourself. This is an act of courage and an act of self-love.

Returning to the quote at the beginning of this chapter, Thich Nhat Hanh says that handling a strong emotion is a lot like taking care of a crying baby. When a baby is crying, what does a loving and skillful parent do? Does the parent blame the baby or get upset at the baby? Does the parent just ignore the baby's cries? No—the baby might cry even more. Instead, a loving and skillful parent will pick up the crying baby. Just holding the baby will bring some relief to the parent as well as to the baby. Then, the parent will pay careful attention to the baby and try to understand what is going on for him or her. When the parent sees clearly what the baby wants or needs, the parent can respond appropriately—for example, by feeding the baby or changing his or her diaper.

You can hold your own difficult emotions the same way. With self-compassion, you can hold the pain within your own heart—looking at it tenderly, accepting it, and making peace with it. With beginner's mind, you can examine your emotion with curiosity, to learn more about it and about yourself. You can smile to yourself, to help awaken your compassion and reengage your human brain. Then, you will be able to see the situation more clearly and respond more wisely.

Try This! Move, Belly Breathe, Embrace

Try this three-step practice the next time you feel a strong difficult emotion arising. You don't have to do the three steps in order. In certain situations, you might choose to do just one or two of the steps instead of all three. Experiment with the practice until you learn from your own experience what is most helpful for you.

Before you begin, mindfully STOP (see chapter 7): Stop what you are doing. Take three mindful breaths. Observe and recognize that stress and strong emotion are present right now. Silently identify the emotion to yourself—for example, *Anger is present,* or *Panic is present*. Then, instead of automatically acting on that emotion, make an intentional choice to take care of yourself and your emotion.

Step 1: Move Your Body

Go for a mindful walk for ten or twenty minutes. Or practice some mindful movement (see chapter 8). Or put on your headphones and dance, or go for a mindful run or bike ride. Do any kind of exercise that you prefer. As best you can, stay in the present moment. Every time your mind gets flooded with stressful thoughts, like *This sucks!* or *I can't stand this!* just bring your full awareness back to each step, each movement, and each breath.

Step 2: Belly Breathe

When you are ready to be still, find a place where you can sit or lie down quietly for a few minutes. If you decide to sit, hold yourself tall and stable, like a mountain. If you choose to lie down, lie on your back. Feel the floor or cushion underneath you, aware of the earth supporting you.

Imagine that you are a tree. Your head is the top of the tree—all the branches and leaves. This is the most vulnerable part of the tree, the part that gets blown around wildly in the wind. Your belly or lower abdomen is the trunk of the tree. This is the strongest part of the tree, solidly rooted in the earth. Imagine that the emotion that threatens to overwhelm you is an approaching storm. As the storm begins to whip your leaves and branches (your thoughts) around, focus all your attention and awareness on your trunk. Mentally embrace the trunk of your tree—imagine this is the area just below your belly button.

To start belly breathing, reconnect with your breath: *Breathing in, I know that I am breathing in. Breathing out, I know that I am breathing out. In… Out…*

Then, place one hand gently on your lower belly, just below your belly button (this is the trunk of your tree). Place your other hand on your chest. Notice the difference between your chest moving and your belly moving. Do you feel your chest rising and falling with each breath? Do you feel your belly button moving in and out with each breath? Which one is moving more—your chest or your belly button?

Continue to follow your breath, gradually bringing your breath down lower into your belly. Allow your belly to fill up with each breath, and let your chest become more still with each breath. As best you can, bring all of your aware-ness to the way the hand resting gently on your lower belly moves in and out with each breath. Your chest should barely move at all.

You might want to also imagine that there is a large, round balloon in your belly, inflating slowly as you breathe in and deflating slowly as you breathe out. You could also experiment with counting *One—two—three—four* as you inflate your belly, and again as you deflate your belly. Ride the waves of emotion as you breathe in and out deeply in your belly.

Remember that an emotion is just an emotion. You can survive any strong emotion that arises. Remind yourself that strong emotions, just like powerful storms, never last forever. Know that as long as you stay connected to this strongest part of yourself, you will be safe. Take shelter in your trunk, con-tinue breathing deeply from your belly, and allow the storm to pass.

Step 3: Embrace Your Emotion

As your emotional storm starts to subside, you can make a mindful choice to soothe and heal that emotion with compassionate awareness.

As best you can, accept the emotion fully. Stay with it compassionately, for as long as you can. As best you can, keep your awareness on the emotion as a physical sensation, or on the way it expresses itself in your body. Try to embrace it with gentleness and kindness, like a loving mother holding a crying baby.

Name the emotion, and smile to it with self-compassion. For example, *Breathing in, I am aware of sadness. Breathing out, I smile to my sadness. Aware of sadness… Smiling…* (Nhat Hanh 2009, 7). If you don't know what to call the emotion, you can simply call it *emotion* or *feeling*. Give yourself permission to feel it, saying to yourself silently as you breathe, *It's okay—it's already here* (Segal, Williams, and Teasdale 2013, 278). Hold your difficult emotion with great care, breathing with it mindfully.

The intent of this practice isn't for you to force yourself to feel a certain way or to feel "better." It is simply for you to be awake to yourself and your own experience, with self-compassion and an open heart. Observe how the difficult emotion changes over time—how it ebbs and flows, like the weather, or like waves in the ocean. Breathe with it for as long as you need to—five minutes, ten minutes, twenty minutes, or more. When you feel ready, carry on with your day, staying as mindful as you can.

In the end, there is no avoiding difficult emotions. Sadness, anger, and anxiety will inevitably arise in your life. How you relate to them, however, is totally up to you. Mindfulness can help you discover your own power to handle difficult emotions. You don't need to "get rid" of difficult emotions, but you can transform your relationship with them. You don't need to be afraid of them. You don't need to turn away from them. You can embrace your difficult emotions and handle them with awareness and self-compassion. When you do, you will free yourself from a tremendous amount of stress and discover your true resilience.

Chapter 11

Handling School Stress

Meditation practice isn't about trying to throw ourselves
away and become something better. It's about
befriending who we are already.

— Buddhist nun Pema Chödrön (1996, 3)

Is school exceedingly stressful for you? Do you experience a
lot of pressure from your teachers, from your family, or from
yourself? If so, you already have the tool you need! More
and more, teachers and students are discovering the power
of mindfulness. Mindfulness is already practiced in the
classroom and after school at hundreds of schools throughout
the world. It helps both students and teachers handle stress,
get along and communicate better, and pay attention and
perform better in the classroom. You might not think of your
school as a place to practice mindfulness. But, if you practice
creatively, you might discover many ways to be mindful at
school and to free yourself from unnecessary stress.

✳ *Melissa's Story*

Melissa had been missing a lot of school, about two or three days every week, because of stress. "I sit in class, and then I start getting freaked out," she said. "I start panicking, and my stomach starts hurting. Then I have to get up and leave the classroom." Most of the time, she would go home. The more school she had missed, the more she had fallen behind in her classes, and the more she had gotten stressed out. It was starting to get so bad that some days she had been too stressed out to even go to school. She also had started to miss volleyball practice and even games, which made her more stressed out, because she loved volleyball so much, and because playing sports helped her manage stress.

After about four weeks of learning and practicing meditation in the mindfulness course, Melissa made a remarkable discovery. She said, "I was sitting in class, and I started freaking out again. But this time, I remembered that there was something that I could do. Instead of freaking out and leaving, I remembered that I could just try breathing." She practiced a sitting meditation for three minutes, right there in the school classroom. She didn't tell anyone that this was what she was doing—she simply practiced following her breath, breathing from her belly, and returning to the present moment every time a wave of stress came over her. "That was the first time in a really long time that I didn't get up and leave," she said proudly. She had stayed in school for the rest of the day.

By the end of the eight-week mindfulness course, Melissa shared, "I haven't missed school in the last four weeks. Every time I started to freak out, I knew I could do something. I knew I could just meditate."

Homework and Exam Stress

Have you ever sat down to do your homework, only to find that you just could not concentrate or focus? Have you ever sat down for an exam and gotten so stressed that you couldn't remember a single thing, even though you had studied and prepared? Or maybe you got lost in thoughts and stories about the future or about the past. For example, *I'm going to fail this test. I'm going to fail this class. What if I don't get into college? Or I should have studied more. What's wrong with me?*

When your mind goes blank or gets pulled away from the present moment by a stressful train of thought, that is a sure sign that your old friend, your lizard brain, is getting activated. Remember, your lizard brain isn't designed to learn algebra or remember who won the War of 1812—it's designed to help you survive being attacked by a tiger!

The good news is you can get off of that train and calm your lizard brain. Practice mindfully STOPping (see chapter 7). Just a few mindful breaths can help you come back to the present moment, reengage your human brain, and let go of stress. The SOBER Breathing Space (also from chapter 7) is another short, practical tool that can help you be at your best at school.

—————————Teen Voices: *Nicole T.*—————————

"[One day, r]ight before a test, I was really stressed out. So I went to the washroom and did a three-minute SOBER Coping Space. That was really helpful. And I actually did better on the test than I would have... The rumination of *I'm going to fail; I'm going to do really badly on this test; they're going to judge me for doing really badly on this test; I'm not ready...* It all kind of slowed down, and I was able to look at it in a more reasonable kind of way. The breathing really helped. I got a lot calmer... I was able to get through the questions and not stress out about every little thing that could go wrong."

Try This! The SOBER Breathing Space for School Stress

The next time you sit down to take a test, to study, or to do homework, practice the SOBER Breathing Space (as outlined below) before you start.

1. **Stop.** Put down your pencil, close your book, or put your computer on standby.

2. **Observe.** Is stress present for you right now? If so, how does that stress feel in your body? Are you noticing stressful thoughts, like *I'm so stupid! I hate doing homework*, or *This assignment sucks*? Are you distracted by some other difficulty in your life? Whatever you are feeling right now is okay. As best you can, accept this moment, just as it is.

3. **Breathe.** For the next minute, allow your attention to rest gently on just your breath. Get off of that stressful train of thought, and give yourself a mindful break from rumination.

4. **Expand.** Expand your awareness. Check in again with your body sensations, your emotions, and your thoughts. Is your stress response still activated in your mind or body? Is your mind any clearer now?

5. **Respond.** Respond to the situation mindfully, with awareness and a self-compassionate intention. With the next breath, bring your awareness back to the classroom, back to your studies, or back to your assignment. Just do that one activity with your full attention. Turn that activity into an informal mindfulness practice—for example, "homework meditation" or "writing meditation"—staying openhearted and present. See whether working more mindfully helps you let go of stress and think more clearly. And, if stress reappears, remember that mindfulness is only one breath away.

Bringing Mindfulness into Your School Day

You can practice informal mindfulness throughout your day at school, as often as you want. It might seem weird at first to be mindful at school. But, you don't have to announce out loud, "I'm practicing mindfulness right now!" Just bringing kindhearted awareness to certain moments throughout your school day, quietly and to yourself, is enough.

Try This! Walking Meditation at School

The next time you walk from one classroom to another, turn it into a walking meditation. Take three or four steps with every in-breath and every out-breath. Bring your awareness to each step and each breath. Notice your surroundings—the sounds and sights in the school hallways. If you feel weird, nervous, self-conscious, or worried about what people might be thinking, you can simply bring your awareness to that, too.

Come back to the present moment with every step and with every breath. If you are ruminating about what just happened in your last class or worrying about what might happen in your next class, simply notice that and let it go. As best you can, just be present with each step and each moment as you make your way to the next classroom.

See whether practicing mindfulness in this way helps you arrive at the next classroom feeling less stressed, more refreshed, and readier to engage and perform at your best.

Try This! Bells of Mindfulness at School

In chapter 7, you learned how to find bells of mindfulness in your environment. It turns out that schools are full of mindfulness bells! Here are a few:

- School bell

- Class bell

- Lunch bell

- People's cell phones ringing

Can you think of any more sounds that you hear at school that you can use as bells of mindfulness?

When you hear one of these bells of mindfulness at school, that is an invitation to mindfully STOP: Stop whatever it is that you were doing—for example, stop walking down the hall, close your book, or put your pencil down. Let go of thoughts about the past, let go of stress about the future, and return to the present moment. Enjoy three mindful breaths. Check in with what is happening right now, both inside you and around you. Then, when you are ready, carry on with whatever you were doing, with mindfulness and awareness.

Stress and Perfectionism: Learning to Embrace Your Mistakes

Mindfulness and self-compassion involve letting go: letting go of the need to be perfect and letting go of the fear of mistakes. I learned a lot about letting go of perfectionism by studying and playing jazz piano. Jazz is improvisational—you don't write out all the notes ahead of time, and you don't know how a performance will sound until you actually play it. For me, playing jazz is a mindfulness practice—I have to be fully in the moment, with open ears and an open heart. When I'm improvising with other musicians, I can't think about the past or the future, or else I'll miss what is happening in the moment.

When I first started learning to play jazz, I was very afraid of making mistakes. I was scared of what my teachers, or the other musicians, might think of me. I wanted everything I played to be perfect. Eventually, though, I came to find that my perfectionism took the life, beauty, and meaning out of the music.

As a teenager, you might be feeling a lot of pressure from your parents, your teachers, your principal, and your coaches. They might be telling you that you have to be perfect all the time—that you're not allowed to make mistakes. You have to get straight A's, be the top athlete, be the best at your extracurricular activities, and be the perfect son, daughter, sister, or brother.

But it is impossible to never make mistakes, and it is impossible to be good at everything. The pursuit of perfection can cause a lot of stress. Believing that you must never make mistakes will make you afraid to try anything new or different, which will limit how much you can learn and grow. The critical voice in your head will keep you mired in self-doubt. Ironically, trying to be perfect actually gets in the way of being successful and reaching your full potential!

Of course, you should always do your best. But, when mistakes happen, as they inevitably will, it's important that you tap into your inner resilience. Resilience is about welcoming your mistakes, learning from them, forgiving yourself, and bouncing back. Making mistakes can help you be more creative, be more productive, and figure out things you never would learn otherwise.

From the point of view of a jazz musician, there is no such thing as a mistake. In a 2010 interview, legendary jazz pianist Herbie Hancock described how he learned this lesson as a young musician just starting out, while playing a concert with Miles Davis's band: "We had the audience in the palm of our hands. And right as everything was really peaking, and Miles was soloing, I played this chord, and it was completely wrong!

"And Miles took a breath and then played some notes, and the notes made my chord right... Somehow, what he chose to play fit my chords to the structure of the music. What I learned from that is that Miles didn't hear the chord as being wrong. He just heard it as something new that happened. So, he didn't judge it. I learned the importance of being nonjudgmental, taking what happens and trying to make it work. That's something you should apply to life, too."

Miles Davis is widely quoted as saying, "Do not fear mistakes: there are none." Every "mistake" is an opportunity to listen deeply and respond creatively. With self-compassion and loving-kindness, you can accept your mistakes and forgive yourself. You don't need to try to be perfect or to "do everything." If you chase after goals every second of every day, you'll never be happy. Happiness is possible only when you stop chasing and cherish the present moment just as it is. Cherish yourself just as you are. You are already a wonder.

Try This! Handling Perfectionism with Mindfulness

The pressure to be perfect comes in many voices. It can be a self-critical voice, saying *I'm not good enough,* or *I'm not smart enough.* Or it can be a voice of fear, asking *What if I mess up?* or *What if I don't do well enough on this test?*

What does the voice of perfectionism sound like for you?

The next time you hear the voice of perfectionism in your mind, just notice it. You don't need to fight it. As best you can, simply allow it to be there, with a sense of curiosity and kindness. Recognize it, and breathe with it. Embrace it, with mindfulness. You can say to yourself, *Breathing in, I recognize my perfectionist voice. Breathing out, I smile.*

You can imagine the voice of perfectionism as an old and familiar friend and perhaps make peace with it. *Hello, my little perfectionist voice. I recognize you. I'm not going to fight you. I know you are there right now, and I will take good care of you.* Then, observe carefully how that inner voice feels in your body. Stay with that sensation, continuing to breathe with it mindfully.

When you can befriend your perfectionist voice with loving-kindness and compassion, it will begin to lose its power over you. You will start to be free of the stress that it can cause.

Teen Voices: *Jane*

"I think that every school should have a mindfulness club. We stress so much at school, it would be really helpful."

144

With the practices of mindful walking, STOPping, the SOBER Breathing Space, and informal mindfulness, the classroom or the school hallway can become your meditation hall. Through awareness and self-compassion, you will begin to gain power over your school stress and your perfectionism. Why not start freeing yourself from school stress by experimenting with one short mindfulness practice at school every day for the next week? As your confidence grows, try practicing mindfulness in more situations throughout your school day.

Chapter 12

Building Mindful Friendships and Romantic Relationships

[A human being] experiences himself, his thoughts and feelings as something separated from the rest [of humanity and nature]—a kind of optical delusion of his consciousness. This delusion is a kind of prison for us... Our task must be to free ourselves from this prison by widening our circle of compassion to embrace all living creatures and the whole nature in its beauty.

— twentieth-century physicist
Albert Einstein
(quoted in Sullivan 1972)

Much of your stress may come from feeling disconnected, isolated, and separated from the people around you. Finding healthy ways of connecting with people can help protect you from stress. You've already learned how mindfulness practice helps you be more present with yourself. In this chapter, you will learn how to bring mindfulness to your friendships and romantic relationships. Then, in the next chapter, you'll learn how you can practice mindfulness to handle stress and conflict with others.

What would healthy friendships and relationships look like for you? What would it look like if you had more connection, more respect and happiness, and less stress in your relationships with friends, family members, and boyfriends or girlfriends?

We're All in This Together: A Network of Interconnectedness

Have you ever noticed that being around classmates, teachers, and family members who are stressed out can make you feel stressed also? On the flip side, have you noticed that when you hang out with people who are happy and relaxed, you tend to feel more happy and relaxed yourself? Stress and happiness are not purely individual matters. Stress is contagious, and so is happiness.

If you closely observe your relationships and your interactions, you can start to see that your well-being is deeply interconnected with the well-being of the people around you. This means that your stress and your happiness have a lot to do with the stress and happiness of the people around you.

So when you practice mindfulness to handle stress, you don't practice just for yourself. Your mindful presence can help your friends and family also. The benefits to you will multiply, because when people in your life are less stressed, you will also be less stressed.

At the heart of loving-kindness—the wish that you and others in your life may enjoy peace, happiness, and wellness—is the insight that we are all interconnected. You were born with the spirit of loving-kindness, and, with gentle intention and practice, you can cultivate and strengthen it. When you have learned how to care for yourself with loving-kindness, you will have created the foundation for relating to other people mindfully. You can then extend your mindfulness and compassion into your relationships with other people.

Try This! Loving-Kindness Meditation

You can do this mindfulness practice using the instructions below or with the help of the recording (track 10) available at http://www.newharbinger .com/30802.

In this meditation, you will be invited to silently repeat a few phrases or wishes in the spirit of loving-kindness. You will send these wishes first to yourself, then to someone you feel close to, then to someone you have neutral feelings for, then to someone you have difficulty with, and finally to all beings in the entire universe. As you practice this meditation, don't try too hard to feel anything in particular. As best you can, just allow your heart to open, and allow the wishes to resonate. Observe closely whatever arises inside of you.

Start by sitting quietly and comfortably, or lying down on your back if you prefer. Notice that you are breathing, right now in this moment. At this moment, there is nothing else for you to do and nowhere for you to go—there is only this breath and this moment.

Picture yourself, in as much detail as you can. Concentrate on this mental image, aware that the very foundation of loving-kindness is self-compassion. As you do so, say the following phrases silently to yourself, in the spirit of loving-kindness:

- *May I be happy.*

- *May I be well.*

- *May I be free from suffering.*

- *May I be at peace.*

Take three slow, mindful breaths. What feelings are you experiencing right now? Where do you feel them in your body?

Now let go of the image of yourself, and bring to mind a person or being you feel close and connected to. This could be a family member, your best friend, the person you are dating right now, or perhaps a pet. Take a moment to really bring this person or being into your mind's eye. Silently send loving-kindness to that person:

- *May you be happy.*

- *May you be well.*

- *May you be free from suffering.*

- *May you be at peace.*

Take three slow, mindful breaths. Again, notice what arises. As best you can, be patient and kind with yourself, without expecting yourself to feel any certain way.

Now let go of the image of this person you feel close to, and bring to mind someone you are not very strongly connected to—like a classmate, teacher, or neighbor whom you don't know very well. Although you are not strongly connected to this person, you may recognize that because you are inter-connected, this person's well-being relates in some small way to your own well-being. Send this person the same wishes with loving-kindness: *May you be happy. May you be well. May you be free from suffering. May you be at peace.*

Now let go of the image of this person you are not strongly connected to, and bring to mind someone who has caused you difficulty. (The first time you do this practice, it would be best to bring someone to mind with whom you have only a relatively small or minor conflict.) Aware of your intercon-nectedness with this person, you can see that the more stress and pain that person experiences, the more difficulty that person is going to cause for *you*. In the same way, you can see that if this person were able to handle his or her stress better and enjoy some more happiness and well-being, it might make *your* life better also. Experiment with sending loving-kindness to this person: *May you be happy. May you be well. May you be free from suffering. May you be at peace*. This may feel easy or difficult, natural or awkward. Just notice that as you breathe.

Finally, bring to mind all beings in your community. Gradually broaden this image to include all beings in your city, your country, and the world. We are all connected in a network of interdependence. Your stress and your happi-ness are, to some extent, related to the stress and happiness of all beings on the planet. Practice extending your circle of compassion to embrace the entire universe: *May all beings be happy. May all beings be well. May all beings be free from suffering. May all beings be at peace.*

What did you notice as you sent well wishes to yourself, then to other people or beings in your life?

Although it may be easy to offer loving-kindness to someone with whom you have a good relationship, it is usually harder to send loving-kindness to someone who has caused you difficulty. Or, you might find it difficult to send loving-kindness to yourself. You can experiment with variations on the loving-kindness meditation above. For example, you can switch up the order of the meditation and start by offering loving-kindness to someone you are close to. Many teens find it easiest to start by sending loving-kindness to their pet dog or cat. You might consider skipping—for now—the part about offering loving-kindness to someone with whom you have difficulty. You can also make up your own phrases and wishes, if you want.

Just like everyone else, I get angry sometimes. In my own experience, holding on to anger and resentment toward someone else mostly just makes *me* more stressed out, and it doesn't make the situation any better. I've found that the most useful thing to do is let go of my anger toward that person and try to wish him or her well. Not because the other person deserves it, but because *I* deserve it! It may or may not make a difference to the other person if I do this, but it helps me feel less stressed and more peaceful. Usually, once my anger has subsided, I can deal with that person and resolve the situation in a better way.

One time, I was *really* angry at someone for several years because he did many things that were really hurtful. I practiced sending him loving-kindness over and over again, for months. Eventually, I came to see that he behaved the way that he did mostly because he had so much fear in his heart. He was afraid, and he was trying to protect himself and the people he cared about by attacking others. Even though what he was doing still wasn't fair, I was at least better able to understand why he was acting that way. Once I saw this clearly, my anger and resentment toward him gradually turned into compassion. Instead of staying angry at him, I just wanted him to be happier and less afraid, so that he could start acting more peacefully. This compassion was good medicine for me, because it helped me spend less time and energy ruminating and complaining about him and more time and energy enjoying my own life.

When practicing loving-kindness meditation, it's important to be patient with yourself. Cultivating your innate loving-kindness is like watering a seed. You may need to keep at it for a while before you see results, but, during that time, the seed has germinated and roots are growing. After a few weeks, or a few months, you may be delighted to discover that a beautiful flower has bloomed in your heart.

Mindful Communication: Offering Your True Presence

Have you ever been having a conversation with your best friend or girlfriend or boyfriend and felt that he or she wasn't really listening to you? That he or she was physically with you, but mentally "checked out," thinking about something else, not really "there"? Maybe he or she was too busy texting to really pay attention to you. How did that feel?

When you truly care for someone, the most precious gift that you can offer him or her is not money, jewelry, or a fancy dinner. The most precious gift you can offer someone is not even a "thing" at all—it is just being fully there with him or her, 100 percent, in the moment. When you are present with someone with loving-kindness and an open heart, the quality of your presence alone can be refreshing.

When you are truly there for yourself and the other person, you can practice mindful communication, which consists of *deep listening* and *compassionate speech. Deep listening* involves doing your best to listen with an open mind and open heart. One thing we all have in common is that we want to feel heard and understood. When you practice deep listening, you listen just to really hear and understand the other person as best you can. You try not to judge what he or she is saying as "right" or "wrong." You try not to interrupt him or her, correct him or her, or attempt to "fix" his or her problem. You just listen. Especially when that person is stressed or upset, your compassionate presence alone can be soothing. This is an act of true friendship, of true love.

Compassionate speech involves being deeply aware of what you are saying as you say it. It also involves speaking with the primary intention of helping the other person be well, be happy, and be at peace. When you practice compassionate speech, you try to avoid saying things that might cause unnecessary stress, hurt, or difficulty. In fact, mindful communication is less about knowing what to say than knowing what *not* to say.

If you are currently experiencing a lot of stress in your conversations and relationships, mindful communication can be a powerful antidote to conflict. The next time you are hanging out with your best friend or your girlfriend or boyfriend—for example, having a meal, going for a walk, or enjoying a cup of coffee—why not practice the art of deep listening and compassionate speech, to get a feel for it?

Try This! Deep Listening and Compassionate Speech

Any time you wish to try some mindful communication, first practice mindfully STOPping: Stop whatever you are saying and doing, and shift out of autopilot. Turn off your cell phone, your TV, and any other electronic devices, so that you can be fully present. Breathe in and out mindfully three times. Recognize how precious this moment is, this chance to be with your friend or loved one. Notice what is happening within you: are you stressed, angry, anxious, depressed, or happy? Notice, too, what seems to be happening within the other person. You don't need to tell the other person that you are about to start practicing mindfulness. Simply embody as best you can the mindful spirit of beginner's mind, self-compassion, and loving-kindness as you enter into deep listening.

Allow the person to share with you whatever is on his or her mind. You may wish to ask a few simple questions, like "What's going on?" or "How was your day today?" But your primary intention is just to listen. With beginner's mind, listen as if you've never met this person before. Can you learn something new about this person or understand him or her in a new way? Can you listen without interrupting, without judging, and without planning what you're going to say next?

Notice what is happening inside of you as you listen. If stress arises as you listen, just notice it and breathe. If an urge to interrupt, to judge, or to give advice comes up, just notice it and breathe.

As the conversation unfolds, practice compassionate speech. Speak mindfully, aware that what you say and how you say it has the power to deeply affect the other person. Bring awareness to your own emotions as you speak. Slow down, and pay attention to what you say as you talk. As best you can, use words and language that might help the other person feel comfortable, understood, and cared for. The practice of conscious smiling and breathing can be really helpful here. If you breathe mindfully and smile gently as you speak, your words will naturally convey compassion and loving-kindness, without you having to try too hard or do anything special.

✳ *Roxanne's Story*

Roxanne had been dating her boyfriend for six months, and things were going pretty well between them. But she said she had noticed that whenever she was stressed out, they had a tendency to get into petty arguments.

Roxanne shared that after she practiced mindful listening and mindful speech with her boyfriend for a few weeks, "My boyfriend actually noticed the difference before I did. He said that I've been more present with our conversations. It had made a difference for him. He found out that I was more 'there' when we were together, listening to him instead of trying to redirect what he was trying to say.

"Other people have noticed it too," Roxanne continued. "It's made a difference for my best friend, too, when we hang out together and I can be more mindful."

Because stress is contagious, and your happiness is connected to the happiness of others, your mindfulness practice isn't a purely individual matter. You don't just practice mindfulness for yourself—your mindfulness practice has the power to help the people around you as well as reduce stress in your relationships. Listening and speaking mindfully, with loving-kindness, can be a great way to support the people you care about and strengthen your sense of connection with them, as well as your own resilience to stress.

Chapter 13

Handling Conflict with Other Teens

Raise your words, not your voice. It is rain
that grows flowers, not thunder.

— thirteenth-century poet
Jalal ad-Din ar-Rumi

Conflict with other teens, such as arguments, bullying, and
peer pressure, can be a huge source of stress in your life. It can
make you angry, anxious, and afraid. If you don't know how
to handle it, you can end up saying or doing things that you
don't want to do.

Mindfulness can help you handle stressful situations like
these. Instead of reacting out of frustration or fear and
possibly making things worse, you can stop and take care of
your own emotions. Then, you can make a mindful choice to
handle the situation in a way that is better both for you and for
those around you.

✳ Emily's Story

Emily shared that she experienced stress at school, with other teens in her grade. She had been getting into a lot of arguments, including with her best friend. "There's always so much drama with my friends," she told us. "They're always saying stupid stuff!"

During the fourth week of the mindfulness course, Emily learned the art of mindful communication—mindful listening and compassionate speech. The following week, she told us that she hadn't had to wait very long for an opportunity to practice mindful communication in a stressful situation. During a conversation with her friend, who was talking about how upset she was about a recent argument with another one of their friends, Emily had started to feel irritated. But, because of her mindfulness, she noticed right away that she was getting stressed out. She noticed the urge to argue with her friend. Instead of acting on that urge, she remembered to practice mindfully STOPping because, as she said, "I had been doing the practice so often that it was stuck in my mind."

Emily practiced just listening, just being with her friend, without saying anything right away. After taking a few mindful breaths, she told her friend, "I'm here to listen, not to argue... I'm just noticing that you're saying these things, but I'm not taking offense by it."

I asked Emily what happened next and whether it was any different than how it usually would have been. Emily answered, "This was very different—very, very different! Before, there would have been so much drama, [and] swearing at each other. Then there would have been a big rivalry afterward." Instead, she had been able to bring mindfulness to that moment with her friend, avoid an argument, and help both of them feel less stressed and more at peace.

Handling Conflict with People Close to You

Have you ever, in a moment of anger, told someone something that you didn't really mean? For example, "I hate you," or "I don't ever want to talk to you again"? Maybe you didn't even realize what you were saying at the time. Perhaps you were just reacting without thinking, on autopilot.

How might things have gone differently if your lizard brain hadn't been in control in that situation? What might have happened differently if you had been more aware of what you were saying in that moment?

In chapter 12, you learned how practicing the art of mindful communication can enhance your friendships, your romantic relationships, and your connection with others in general. Mindful communication can also help you transform a difficult situation or an argument or other conflict. With mindfulness, you will be more in touch with your own inner wisdom, and you'll know what to say and what not to say to handle the difficulty and reduce the tension.

Try This! STOP and Communicate Mindfully When Things Get Difficult

The next time a friend of yours says or does something that makes you feel stressed or irritated or pressured, instead of reacting right away, practice mindfully STOPping: Don't say or do anything. Instead, come back "home," to the present moment. Take three breaths to give yourself a space between your stress and your reaction, an opportunity to find a more skillful response. Observe what is happening inside you. If stress or judgment or irritation is arising, simply recognize it for what it is. For example, say silently to yourself, *Stress is arising*, or *Irritation is present*. The simple act of recognizing the feeling and naming it will help calm your lizard brain. Continue to breathe with this awareness. When you feel ready, proceed with mindful communication.

Practice deep listening—just being present with your friend. Your friend might be saying things that are upsetting to you or aren't completely true. Perhaps you can recognize that the reason your friend is saying these things is because his or her own lizard brain is activated. In other words, your friend might not be thinking things through. If you try to interrupt or correct your friend, he or she may not be able to process what you are saying, and it might just activate his or her lizard brain even more. Maybe you will have a chance to say what's on your mind later, when things are calmer. But, for now, as best you can, listen just for the sake of listening. Maybe what your friend needs right now, more than anything, is just to feel heard. Try to listen without interrupting and without mentally passing judgment. When stress or irritation starts to arise inside of you, recognize it and breathe with it.

As you listen, continue to follow your breath. Focusing on your breath can protect you from becoming overwhelmed by "secondhand stress," even if your friend's words are full of blame or judgment. Perhaps your mindful presence will start to rub off on your friend, helping him or her be more mindful also.

Remember that mindful communication is also about knowing what *not* to say. Before you say anything—before you respond or answer a question—check in with yourself: Where are your voice and your words coming from in this moment? Are they coming from stress, judgment, or irritation? Is your own lizard brain activated? In such moments, it might be better to not say anything right away. Instead, just continue to listen and mindfully follow your breath, as best you can.

If what you're about to say comes from a place of calm, ask yourself the following questions. (This common advice, which fits with Buddhist teachings, may come from a poem by Mary Ann Pietzker, published in 1872.)

- Is what you're about to say *true*? If you say something that you're not sure is true, you're likely to cause more stress for yourself and the other person.

- Is what you're about to say *kind*? Is saying it going to be faithful to your intention to practice mindful compassion?

- Is what you're about to say *necessary and helpful to say right now*? Is the other person capable of processing it in this moment, while his or her lizard brain is activated? Or would it be more helpful later, after things have cooled down?

Instead of automatically saying what's on your mind just because you feel as if you have to say something, you can make a mindful choice not to say anything at all. Sometimes, just listening is enough. Sometimes, silence is more powerful and healing than words. Sometimes, the most compassionate thing you can do when your friend is hurting and upset is to just be with him or her.

If you choose to say something, practice compassionate speech. As best you can, choose words that will help the other person feel heard and understood, not blamed or judged. Take a mindful breath between sentences, which can curb impulsive and hurtful remarks and create space for a more kind and compassionate response.

A common practice is to use *I-statements* to express yourself honestly, clearly, and kindly. For example:

- "I see that you're really upset right now."

- "I felt hurt when I didn't get a call back from you."

- "Thanks for telling me about that. I really want to understand how that made you feel."

- "I don't want to do that right now."

It might also be helpful to avoid or minimize your use of *You-statements*, such as "You should have done this," or "You shouldn't have said that." In stressful situations, You-statements can make the other person feel blamed or attacked, which might trigger his or her lizard brain more and make the situation more stressful.

Handling stressful conversations with mindfulness and skill can be really challenging. It's important to be mindful of your own capacity to practice this. If your lizard brain is getting activated and you feel as though you can't continue to listen mindfully and nonjudgmentally, that's okay. There's no need to judge yourself. A wise and compassionate response might be to tell your friend, "I'm feeling pretty stressed right now; I need to take a break. Can we talk about this later?" Then, practice mindful walking or mindful sitting, and take care of your own stress with self-compassion.

And when you do make a mistake and say something unmindful or hurtful, remember to forgive yourself. Remember that you deserve that kindness just as much as anyone else.

When Stress Turns to Anger

Arguments and fights with other kids can be really stressful. If you get bullied, harassed, or intimidated—at school, at sports practice, or in your neighborhood—the intense stress can quickly lead to anger. There's nothing wrong with anger, and you have every right to feel angry. But what you *do* with that anger is important.

The most mindful choice in that kind of situation might be to stop and take care of your anger before trying to deal with whoever made you angry. As Thich Nhat Hanh (2001, 24) put it, if someone just set your house on fire, you might be tempted to chase down and punish the person who started the fire, but in the meantime your house would burn down! A better response would be to put out the fire first.

Anger, like fire, can cause a huge amount of damage to yourself and to other people, if you don't know how to handle it. If you let your lizard brain take control when you're angry, you'll likely make things worse. You might end up getting hurt or hurting someone else. Or you might get in trouble at school, at home, or even with the police. Even when you are angry, you can find a mindful response to a difficult situation.

✱ *Elizabeth's Story*

Elizabeth shared how she had been in class at school one day, working on a group project with some other students, when the teacher came over to see how everything was going. One of Elizabeth's classmates lied to the teacher, telling the teacher how much she had been doing for the project, when, in reality, Elizabeth had been doing most of the work.

"I wanted to kill her! I was so mad!" Elizabeth told us. But, instead of getting into a fight, which would only have made things worse, she left the room and did a breathing meditation. As she meditated, she noticed that she was having all kinds of judgmental thoughts about her classmate. "Like Why [was she] doing that? Why [doesn't she] take a mindfulness course?! *I also kept [imagining] what everyone else thought when I left the room. Was everyone wondering what I was doing?*

"I knew I was mad," said Elizabeth. "I said to myself, Okay, that's there. But I'm not going to worry about it. *Instead, I kept bringing it back to my breath. It was hard. But, it helped. I was able to go back to the room feeling much more calm. And I'm glad I didn't get into a fight!"*

Try This! The SOBER Breathing Space for Anger

The next time someone says or does something that makes you angry, give yourself a chance to respond with mindfulness and wisdom. Remove yourself from the situation, if you can do so safely—for example, step out of the room and into the hallway. Then, practice the SOBER Breathing Space (as outlined below) to come back to yourself and take care of your anger so that you can see the situation clearly and respond wisely. You can do this while standing, sitting, or walking.

1. **Stop.** Instead of yelling, slamming a door, or punching a wall, just take a mindful pause.

2. **Observe.** What's happening right now, inside of you? Recognize that anger is present. Notice how the anger feels in your body. Is there a hot sensation? Is your heart racing? Are you breathing faster? Are the muscles in your shoulders or jaw starting to clench?

   Be there for yourself, no matter what is happening. You can even practice compassionate speech toward your lizard brain: *Hello, lizard brain—I recognize you. It's okay, I'll take care of you.*

   Mindfully observe your thinking. Are you ruminating, replaying in your mind over and over what the person said or did to make you angry? Perhaps you keep thinking about what you wish that you had said or done. Is your anger rising the more you ruminate? Remember that you don't have to stay on that angry train of thought. You can get off of that train and come back to the healing power of your own breath. Remember that anger doesn't rule you—you don't have to act on your anger.

3. **Breathe.** Let go of rumination by mindfully bringing your awareness back to your breath, and back to your body, over and over again. For the next minute or so, practice focusing on your breath. Every time you find yourself ruminating about who did what, just notice that you are doing so and come back to your next breath. You can say silently to yourself, *Breathing in, I know that I am breathing in. Breathing out, I know that I am breathing out. In… Out…*

4. **Expand.** Widen your awareness back to your whole body and mind. Is anger still present in your body and mind? If so, that's okay. You can view anger as an invitation to continue to take care of yourself, to continue to practice mindfulness.

5. **Respond.** Depending on how intense your stress is in this moment, you might want to do something that will continue to cool the flames of your anger. You can practice slow or fast mindful walking, prac-

tice mindful movement, or repeat the SOBER Breathing Space. You might choose to go exercise, have a mindful snack, or talk to a friend or family member. Do these things for as long as you need to, with compassion for yourself and maybe even compassion for the person who made you angry. Whether it takes three minutes or three days, you have the right to as much time as you need to take care of yourself and your stress with mindfulness and self-compassion.

Once your human brain is reactivated, you will be able to see the situation more clearly, and you will know how to respond to the situation more skillfully. At that point, you might choose to have a mindful conversation with the person who made you angry, or you might try to get a friend or an adult involved who can help resolve the conflict. In this way, you can handle your anger skillfully and make a wise choice that avoids creating more stress.

Teen Voices

"[Mindfulness has] helped me be a lot more relaxed and not get angry so often, and when I do get angry, it helps me calm down so the anger doesn't get too bad." —Jun

"When I meditate, I feel more relaxed [and] less angry, and I'm able to think more clearly again." —Marcus

"When we're about to get into an argument, we can take three mindful breaths together. We're able to pull each other back." —Xochi

It's important to connect with your peers in a positive and healthy way. Mindfulness can give you enormous power to handle stressful situations with other teens. The next time you are in an argument with your friend, your boyfriend, or your girlfriend, see whether mindfulness can help you find a way out of the difficulty. If you are being bullied or are experiencing pressure to do something you don't want to, remember that you don't have to act on your anger or your fear. You already have the tools you need to help you stop, breathe, listen, think, and respond with more wisdom and compassion.

Chapter 14

Mindful Peacemaking at Home

If you want others to be happy, practice compassion.
If you want to be happy, practice compassion.

— the Dalai Lama

One of the biggest sources of stress for teens is difficulties with family members. (By "family," I mean parents, adoptive parents, foster parents, siblings, grandparents, aunts, uncles, cousins, close family friends—anyone you live with or are really close to, even if you don't always get along.) When communication is tense between you and your parents, everyone at home is unhappy. When you are fighting with your brother or sister, everyone can feel stressed out. When relationships at home are tense, you can end up feeling isolated, which can worsen your stress.

On the other hand, if you can practice mindfulness and compassion in your interactions at home, you can bring a lot of healing, peace, and transformation into your home life. Everyone in your family will benefit.

Teen Voices: *Nicole T.*

"I ignore my little brother all the time. He's thirteen. One day I was like, 'What if he's saying something important, and I'm not listening to it?' So I sat down with him, and we had a conversation, and I was a lot more mindful of what he was saying, and a lot more mindful of what I was saying to him. And we had a really good conversation, and I really enjoyed it. I felt like I was spending quality time with my brother, and it felt really nice... I feel like my relationship is a lot better with him now."

Have you ever noticed that sometimes, your family members—the people you are closest to—can "push your buttons" the most? When a family member does or says something that stresses you out and makes you angry, you might want to blame or punish him or her. If you don't stop to think, before you know it your lizard brain can take over, and you might find yourself yelling, punching a wall, or storming off and slamming your bedroom door. Although such actions might make you feel better in the short term, they can quickly lead to a "toxic" environment. Your home—the place where you should feel most relaxed and safe—can become a place full of stress and conflict.

Cultivating the Heart of Understanding

Mindfulness is about awareness, and it is also about understanding. A misunderstanding with a family member can make you feel stressed out and angry. If you can learn to understand yourself and the other person more deeply, you can correct the misunderstanding and alleviate your stress.

For example, maybe one reason that your mom snapped at you the other night is because she was stressed out. That's not an excuse. But, if you can understand your mom and her situation more, it can help you feel more compassionate and less stressed. Once you really understand your mom's difficulties, you will no longer want to punish her. You will only want her to experience relief. Once she has some relief from her own stress, she will be happier and treat you better. So when you understand her more deeply, compassion for her may arise within you quite naturally as you see clearly that her happiness would benefit both of you.

Any time you're in a conflict, your lizard brain automatically goes into fight, flight, or freeze mode. Your lizard brain tries to prove who is "right" and who is "wrong" by judging whose fault it is and who is to blame. This blocks true understanding and tends to activate your judging mind and your lizard brain even more. The only way to really understand someone is to stay present and listen.

Try This! Mindful Reconciliation

The next time you have a small conflict or disagreement with a family member—for example, your sister borrows something of yours and doesn't return it—as soon as you notice yourself getting stressed or irritated, mindfully STOP. Mindfully STOPping gives you a space to reconnect with your deepest values and intentions. After you breathe mindfully three times, ask yourself, *Is my primary intention here to prove whose fault it is—who "should" do this or "shouldn't" do that? Or, is it to heal and reconcile—to bring more understanding and compassion to the relationship?*

Mindfully STOPping also gives you an opportunity to shift out of fight, flight, or freeze mode. Once you shift into mindful awareness, you might discover ways of handling the situation that would not occur to your lizard brain. You will be better able to think of what can you do and say to help your home life be happier and less stressful. Then, you can practice mindful communication to increase understanding between you and the other person and reconcile the conflict.

Here are some key ingredients in reconciliation and mindful communication, inspired by the "Beginning Anew" practice taught by Thich Nhat Hanh (2009).

Staying present. In your own words, tell the other person something like "I am really here with you right now. I hope that we can work this out." A simple statement like this expresses your mindful presence and compassionate intention. Your mindfulness and compassion might even rub off on the other person. As traditional First Nations wisdom teaches us, "When someone is hurting, just your presence is medicine."

Expressing appreciation. Sometimes when you and another person are experiencing conflict, it can be easy to lose sight of what it is you like or appreciate about that person. Remembering and saying out loud what

174

you appreciate about him or her can restore love and understanding. For example, you might tell your parent, "I know how much you care about me and want me to succeed at school." Speaking in this way will help both you and the other person open your hearts and let go of resentment. (It is important that you be sincere.)

Taking responsibility. As soon as you recognize that you've made a mistake, whether it's big or small, take responsibility for it by apologizing. Apologizing for thoughtlessly saying something hurtful, for example, can relieve the other person's hurt, start to repair the damage, and bring more peace to the situation right away.

You don't need to judge yourself as a "bad" son, daughter, brother, or sister for having made a mistake. You are young, you are learning, and you have a right to make mistakes. But you should take responsibility for the mistakes you make whenever possible. Taking responsibility for your mistakes demonstrates a huge amount of maturity, and the other person may respect you for that. Plus, it paves the way for the other person to take responsibility for his or her own mistakes.

Expressing hurt. Mindful communication involves speaking truthfully and honestly. Don't suppress or ignore your own hurt. Express your hurt using I-statements, and invite the other person to join you in reconciling. For example, you might say, "I felt really upset last night when you yelled at me. I've been upset about it all day. Can we talk about it?" Speak truthfully, sharing what is in your heart, but don't be accusatory. Your primary intention is to heal the relationship, not to judge or blame. Try to look at the difficulty with the other person in order to come to a shared understanding. Use caring language. For example, "I don't understand why you seemed so upset the other night. I'd really like to understand you better. Can you help me understand?" Deep listening is also crucial. Listen to the other person's worries and difficulties, with the intention of understanding him or her better.

Even if you hear something that you don't agree with, just listening can help the other person express pain and release stress. So if you don't understand or agree with what you hear, just continue to follow your breath and, as best you can, continue to listen mindfully instead of arguing back right away. You may have an opportunity to speak up and be heard later, when the situation is more calm.

With practice, you will gain the self-confidence to communicate more skillfully and mindfully in bigger conflicts and arguments, such as when you believe that your parents are expecting too much of you or treating you unfairly. If the problem you need to address is a big one, it might be helpful to ask the other person to agree to talk with you at a time when both of you can be fully present (that is, when you won't feel rushed or busy) and after you've both had a chance to cool off. You might also like to ask for help from a trusted aunt, grandparent, doctor, or counselor who can help you listen to and understand each other. Your combined insight and presence can bring healing to the difficult situation. Reconciliation may take several days and several conversations. Don't rush it.

Taking Care of Yourself First

Mindfulness and compassion don't always involve being nice or saying yes. Sometimes, they involve knowing when you need to take a mindful break, in order to avoid saying or doing something that could make the situation worse. Compassion sometimes involves setting clear boundaries—knowing when to say "No," "I need to go chill out for a little while," or "That's not okay."

When you get on an airplane, the most important safety instruction that the flight attendants give is the one along the lines of "Put your own oxygen mask on before helping your child put on his or hers." They know that if you don't take care of yourself first, you won't be able to help anyone else.

It's the same when handling stressful situations with the people in your life: you need to "put your own oxygen mask on" by breathing and taking care of your own emotions (your irritation, your anger, and so forth) first, before trying to resolve the situation. Use one of the tools that you've learned in this book—the SOBER Breathing Space (chapter 7), mindful movement (chapter 8), or belly breathing (chapter 10)—to help you take care of your own stress with great compassion, like a mother holding a crying baby. Don't be in too much of a rush to talk or to "figure things out." It might be better to wait a day or two, until you've successfully handled your own stress and also given the other person some time to cool off. Taking care of yourself is self-compassion in action. Only when you know how to love yourself will you be capable of truly caring for the people you love.

Teen Voices: *Rachel*

"I had had a really bad day at school. I came home feeling really stressed out. The first thing I decided to do when I got home was sit down and meditate. As I was sitting down, my dad came into my room. He asked me, 'How was your day today?' Without thinking, I blurted out, 'Shut up, I'm trying to be mindful!' My dad is into mindfulness, too. So instead of arguing with me or getting on my case, he just sat down next to me. We meditated together for ten minutes. Then, we ended up having a really nice evening together. I even cooked dinner for my family that night!

"If I hadn't tried to meditate, I'm sure I would have said something even worse to my dad. And if my dad didn't know how to meditate, we probably would have gotten into an argument right away. Instead, we ended up having a really good time together."

Mindful reconciliation with your loved ones is a deep art, and it takes some time and practice. Be patient with yourself, and with everyone else, especially when it seems as if reconciliation isn't working. If cultivating loving-kindness (see chapter 12) is like watering seeds in a garden, so is learning mindful reconciliation. The flowers might not bloom right away, but important changes are taking place beneath the surface. A skillful gardener waters a flower with love and compassion, but without getting too attached to any specific outcome or expectation of how the flower is supposed to look. The Dalai Lama said, "Be kind whenever possible. It is always possible." You always have the power to water the positive seeds in those around you, just by your mindful way of being, breathing, and speaking. Your own deep mindfulness practice can transform your entire family.

Chapter 15

The Power of Mindfulness in Sports, Music, and the Arts

In sports, what gets people's attention is this idea of being in the zone, or playing in the zone... That happens when we are in the moment, when we are mindful of what is going on... When we are in the moment and absorbed with the activity, we play our best.

— sports psychologist George Mumford

It's often said that sports are 90 percent mental and 10 percent physical. The same is true for music, acting, art, and other creative activities. When your mind is wandering and you're not truly present, you're much more likely to miss that three-point shot, or forget your lines in the school play, or not solo as beautifully and passionately as you could. So, it's no wonder that some of the world's top athletes, actors, artists, and musicians—from Michael Jordan to Orlando Bloom to Katy

Perry to Oprah Winfrey—practice meditation. What these people all have in common is that they know how important it is to be present and focused, in the here and now, when they perform.

✱ John's Story

John (a varsity soccer player) shared, "I was skeptical about meditating before my game. I thought I would miss something important. But then I remembered something my coach told me about Phil Jackson, who coached the Chicago Bulls and the Los Angeles Lakers. My coach said that Phil Jackson taught Michael Jordan and Kobe Bryant how to meditate, and that helped them play better.

"So, I decided to try it. I did a two-minute breathing meditation before the game. I didn't miss anything, and I actually ended up playing really well that day! Meditating actually helped me not miss anything and pay attention better."

Being "In the Zone"

Playing music, making art, or engaging in any sport can become a form of meditation, when you do it with your complete attention. Whenever you are fully present with each note you play, each line you draw, or each shot you take, you let go of distractions that would otherwise pull your attention away from your effort.

"Trying too hard" during any of these activities can actually be detrimental. You can't perform at your best when you are distracted by needing to perform a certain way, worrying about what might happen next, feeling bad about your last performance, or being too afraid of making a mistake. Sports psychologist George Mumford (who worked with Phil Jackson in teaching basketball legend Michael Jordan how to meditate) described being "in the zone" as a sense of "effortlessness" or "relaxed concentration." When you are fully in the moment, you don't need to "try" too hard or "do" too much. You are simply fully engaged with what's happening in the present moment, allowing your creativity and talent to flow through you.

George Mumford also said, "This moment is all we've got. It is only in the present moment that we can make changes. And you are not just making these changes for yourself; you are doing it for everyone. Everyone will benefit" (2011). He was referring to that sense of interconnectedness, that "we're all in this together." Your mindfulness helps everyone, and when you take good care of yourself, you are taking good care of others at the very same time. With mindfulness, self-compassion, and loving-kindness, you can let go of the need to win or to be the best. You can simply be fully in the moment— free from stress, pressure, and expectations.

Try This! Informal Meditations in Sports, Music, and the Arts

The next time you step onto the field or the court, or the next time you pick up your paintbrush or instrument, don't jump right into things. Instead, practice mindfully STOPping. Notice whether your mind is wandering, notice where your attention is, and bring yourself 100 percent back to the here and now. Just stop and breathe mindfully until you have arrived in the present moment. Then, proceed with your activity while remembering to stay mindful. Transform the activity into an informal mindfulness practice, a "meditation in motion." Here are some examples:

Stretching meditation. If you are an athlete, you probably stretch and warm up before practices or games. Can you turn this into a "stretching meditation," just like the mindful movement practice that you learned in chapter 8? Can you breathe in and out mindfully with each stretch?

Warm-up meditation. If you are a musician, perhaps you warm up by playing scales. If you are a soccer player, perhaps you warm up by shooting balls into an empty net. Can you turn this activity into a meditation? Can you follow your breath, notice when your mind wanders, and invite yourself back to the here and now with every note, every shot?

Exercising meditation. If you run, bike, swim, or jog, can you transform that routine activity into a time of quiet solitude, peace, and relief from stress? Can you synchronize your movements with your breath, coordinating your body, mind, and heart in rhythm?

Watching and listening meditation. When you are listening to music, can you listen with your whole being? When you are resting on the bench watching your teammates play, can you watch with your whole being? Can you watch and listen without being pulled away into stress, into worries about the future, or into thoughts about the past?

These are just a few examples of meditation practices with sports and arts. Can you come up with your own?

Handling Nerves with Mindfulness

Before a big performance or game, you might experience "butterflies" in your stomach. A little bit of stress during a performance can help focus your attention and give you energy. But, too much stress can paralyze you. If your fight, flight, or freeze response is cranked up, and your lizard brain has taken over, you can no longer think clearly or respond creatively. Your human brain shuts down—your body goes into pure survival mode. You might get a stomachache or even throw up. Or, your mind might go completely blank, unable to remember a thing.

In a moment of extreme stress like this, mindfulness can help you "get out of your own way." You can practice a short formal meditation, such as the SOBER Breathing Space or the body scan, before your big performance or game. Handling pre-performance stress with mindfulness will help you be at your best and help those around you as well.

Teen Voices: *Chloe*

Chloe, a drama student, practiced mindfulness to help her with nerves before rehearsals and performances. For Chloe, the most useful practice was the body scan.

Chloe shared how while preparing for the big school play, she had noticed how nervous everyone was, including herself. The night of the show, the air had been buzzing with stress. So instead of keeping her mindfulness practice to herself, Chloe had decided to share it with her classmates. She said, "I led a body scan meditation with the cast before the show, to calm our nerves. Everyone really liked it, and the show went a lot better!"

Try This! The SOBER Breathing Space or Short Body Scan for Sports, Music, and the Arts

Before your next game or performance, take just a few minutes for yourself. Find a place to sit or lie down. If you have a portable music player and headphones or earbuds, listen to track 4, for the body scan, or track 6, for the SOBER Breathing Space (both available at http://www.newharbin ger.com/30802), or close your eyes and guide yourself through one of the practices as described below. Or, you can play the track out loud and see whether your coach, instructor, or teammates are interested in trying the practice with you, just to see whether it might help you all perform at your best, with less stress.

The SOBER Breathing Space

1. **Stop.** Shift out of autopilot, and enter deeply into the present moment.

2. **Observe.** Simply observe what is happening, with beginner's mind and self-compassion. What is happening right now inside your body? What emotions are arising in you right now? What thoughts are coming up in this moment? You don't need to change, "fix," or judge anything—just observe.

3. **Breathe.** For a minute or so, invite your awareness to rest on only your breath. Give yourself a break from rumination and worries about what might happen during your game or performance. Just ride the waves of your breath. You can say quietly to yourself, *Breathing in, I know that I am breathing in. Breathing out, I know that I am breathing out. In... Out...* Every time your mind wanders, simply notice that: *Hello, wandering mind!* Then, gently bring your awareness back to your breath. You may need to do this repeatedly, and that's okay.

4. **Expand.** Continue to breathe, and expand your awareness back to a sensation of breathing with your whole body. Check in again with what is happening in your body—are there any sensations? Is there any pain? Check in again with your emotions—what feelings are present for you right now? Check in again with your thoughts—what thoughts are arising in your mind right now? Is this moment any different than when you started the practice? Notice the energy inside you and around you.

5. **Respond.** Begin the game or performance as mindfully as you can, confident that your talent and creativity will shine as long as you are present and open.

Five-Minute Body Scan

This is a nice practice to do if you have a place to lie down—for example, backstage or on a bench. Breathe deeply in and out, and focus your attention on each part of your body for about three breaths. You might want to proceed as follows: feet—legs—hips—belly—chest and back—arms—head. Continue to follow your breath, and try to notice any signs of stress in your body, like butterflies in your stomach. Without needing to change or "fix" anything, simply experience those sensations, just as they are. Notice whether anything is different in your mind and body by the time you get up and start your performance.

During either of these short mindful practices, be sure to check in with your thinking. Notice whether your mind is pulled into worries about the future or regrets about the past, such as *What if we lose this game?* or *What if I don't play well?* or *I should have practiced more.* Then, make a mindful choice to get off of that train of thought and come back to the next breath, back to the present moment.

Sports and exercise can be a great way of staying healthy and building positive connections with people. Arts and music can be a powerful source of joy and stress relief. Mindfulness will help you be open to the joys of these activities and also let go of the stress that sometimes comes along with them. Bring mindfulness into your sports, music, and creative hobbies, and transform every action into a meditation. Try it for yourself and allow mindfulness to help you have more fun, perform better, and stress less!

Chapter 16

Mindfulness to Help You Sleep

Feelings come and go like clouds in a windy sky.
Conscious breathing is my anchor.

— Thich Nhat Hanh (1990, 29)

The American Academy of Pediatrics (2014) recommends that teens get eight and a half to nine and a half hours of sleep every night. How much sleep do you get most nights? If you're like most teens, you are chronically sleep-deprived and tired. Getting enough sleep is critical for you to function and learn well and for you to be able to bounce back from stress. The irony is that being too stressed can disrupt your sleep and keep you awake at night, which then makes it more difficult for you to handle stress the next day. Fortunately, mindfulness can help you let go of stress in your mind and body, allowing you to get restful and restorative sleep so that you can handle the next day with confidence.

Your Brain and Body Need Sleep

Have you noticed that when you haven't slept well, you can't think as clearly and you feel grumpy and irritable? Have you noticed that you can't learn as well, concentrate as well, or remember things as well as usual when you're tired? This is because your brain needs good sleep in order to process and remember what you've learned that day and to recover from stress. Sleep deprivation that goes on for weeks, months, or years also puts you at higher risk for mental health problems such as depression and anxiety.

Lack of sleep has huge effects on just about every organ in your body, not just your brain. When you haven't slept well, your energy and strength are lower. This is why professional athletes make a point of getting lots of sleep the night before a big game. Sleep deprivation also affects your immune system, making you more likely to get sick. Missing too much sleep for months or years at a time can even put you at higher risk for all kinds of major health problems, such as diabetes, obesity, and heart disease. So sleeping well is crucial for your health and resilience.

There may be many reasons why you're not getting enough sleep. Maybe you stay up late at night doing homework or hanging out with friends. Maybe you have to get up early in the morning for school or sports practice. Answer the following questions to see whether you are getting enough sleep and whether lack of sleep is affecting your life.

* Do you get less than eight and a half hours of sleep most nights?

* Does it take you more than an hour to get out of bed most mornings?

* Do you feel sleepy during the daytime?

* Do you fall asleep during the day without meaning to, like in class or on the bus?

* Are you often grumpy or irritable when you haven't slept well?

* Do you have difficulty concentrating, remembering, or learning at school because you're so tired?

* Do you often have difficulty falling asleep?

* Does stress or anxiety often keep you awake at night?

* Do you often stay awake at night just lying in bed and thinking about things?

* Do you think that you may be sleep-deprived?

If you answered yes to several of these questions, it could be a sign that you aren't sleeping enough or getting a good quality of sleep. If that's the case, ask yourself: *Do I want to get more sleep? How might getting more sleep benefit me? What is getting in the way of my sleep?*

Maybe you're having difficulty falling asleep. If you lie awake in bed at night, what is it that keeps you up? Is it your own mind—stressful thinking about the past, worrying about the future? Are you simply too stressed out to sleep sometimes?

If so, practicing the body scan at bedtime can help. Although the purpose of the body scan is to help you tune in to your body just the way it is, I've found that good sleep is often a nice "side effect." Practicing the body scan can help you let go of rumination, as well as let go of stress and tension in your body. This then will allow your body to fall asleep by itself, naturally.

Teen Voices: *Paige*

"Through mindfulness, I learned all about being present…, and [I] found the five-minute body scan particularly helpful. It also helped me fall asleep at night when I couldn't relax."

Try This! The Body Scan at Bedtime

Do this mindfulness practice with the help of the recording (track 4 or 11) available at http://www.newharbinger.com/30802.

Every night for the next two weeks, practice a guided body scan at bedtime, as you lie down to sleep. Try a short body scan (track 4), or a longer body scan (track 11) if you have time, like on weekends. Get comfortable in bed, with your head on your pillow, under the covers if you like. Close your eyes and play the track. Allow your attention to rest on your breath, on your body, and on the words of the guided meditation.

You may notice feelings, thoughts, and stress arising in your body and mind as you do the guided meditation. That's okay. Simply allow them to come and go, as if they were clouds in the sky, and then gently bring your attention back to your breath and to your body. This will allow your body to release some of the stress that it has been holding.

If you fall asleep during the meditation, great. If not, that's okay too—after the track ends, check in with your body and your breath. Has anything changed? If you're feeling more relaxed, just enjoy that. If you're still feeling tense and stressed, just notice that without judgment. You don't need to "force" yourself to sleep. Remember that the purpose of doing the body scan isn't necessarily to relax or fall asleep—simply being present with yourself, just as you are, can be healing. It may make a difference for your sleep that night and for your mood and energy the next day.

✳ Lexi's Story

Lexi suffered from chronic stress and anxiety, which kept her awake at night. She told us that sometimes she would stay up for hours in the middle of the night, ruminating about her day, with the result that she was extremely tired the next day. That made it hard for her to pay attention in school, she said, which led to more stress and anxiety.

Lexi later shared that she started listening to guided meditations at night. "It took a while, but after a few days, I was able to go to sleep a lot easier. I felt a lot better the next day, too!"

Sleep Hygiene

When you've been under stress for a long time, your brain can "forget" how to sleep. Perhaps you need to teach your brain how to sleep again. You can do this by following certain guidelines for your sleep environment and your bedtime routine that will help your brain be ready for sleep when you lie down. This is known as "sleep hygiene," and like any other kind of hygiene, it's something that you need to do every day in order to take care of your health. It's kind of like brushing your teeth every morning and night, for good dental hygiene, or practicing mindfulness daily for good mental hygiene (as discussed in chapter 4).

Your sleep environment and what you do in the evenings send powerful messages to your brain about whether or not it should go to sleep. Think about how young children—such as preschoolers—resist their bedtime when there is something fun and exciting they could be doing. They don't want to miss out, even though they're totally exhausted. Your brain can sometimes be like that preschooler who doesn't want to rest. Improving your sleep hygiene involves changing both your sleep environment and your sleep routine in a way that will send the message to your brain, "Nothing is happening. It's boring—there's nothing to do right now but go to sleep."

Try This! Improve Your Sleep Hygiene

Here are some things you can do to help yourself get a good night's sleep (Kelty Mental Health Resource Centre 2011).

Your Sleep Environment: Your Bedroom

If you have a phone, TV, computer, or stereo in your bedroom, move it to another room. If you can't remove all such electronic devices, try at least removing those with screens. Just looking at the light of a screen (for example, on your computer or your phone) activates your brain and disrupts your body's release of the sleep hormone melatonin, making it hard for you to fall asleep even long after the screen is off.

Finally, instead of using your bedroom for everything that you normally do—like hanging out, talking on the phone, using your smartphone or tablet, reading, studying, and doing homework—try to move as many activities as you can into a different room of your home. Try to use your bedroom only for sleeping. If you can use your bedroom just for sleeping, you will send a powerful message to your brain every time you enter your bedroom: *Brain, listen—this room is just for sleeping. There's nothing interesting or fun going on here. It's boring—you won't miss out on anything here—so you can just sleep.*

Your Sleep Routine

Have a consistent sleep schedule. Try to go to bed at the same time and wake up at the same time every day. Aim for at least eight and a half hours of sleep each night. If you need to sleep in late on weekends and other days off to catch up on missed sleep, try not to sleep in for longer than one hour. That's because the more irregular your sleep schedule is, the more confused your brain gets and the harder it is to sleep when you want to.

If you need to take a nap during the day, nap for no longer than sixty minutes. And don't nap in the late afternoon or evening, because if you do, chances are you won't feel sleepy at bedtime.

Have a consistent bedtime routine. About an hour before bedtime, start to wind down your activities. During this time, avoid studying; doing home-work; playing video games; watching TV; using a computer, cell phone, or tablet (anything with a screen); exercising; having intense conversations; and any other activities that might be either stimulating or frustrating. Instead, find quiet and relaxing things to do, like reading an inspiring book, listening to soft music, drinking warm milk or herbal tea, and writing in your journal. Then do the same activities every night, in order to get your brain in the habit of starting to shut down as you get ready to sleep.

These are just a few ideas. If you do a web search for "sleep hygiene," you will find many more. Don't feel as if you have to do everything on this list all at once. Start with one small change that you would like to make right now, and see how it goes for a week. Once you succeed in making that change, your confidence will grow. The following week, you can choose another change to make.

Remember to be patient with yourself. It can take weeks or months to start to change your brain's sleep habits. But, over time, practicing good sleep hygiene is a safe and powerful way to change your brain's sleep patterns. If you continue to have problems with sleep even after making changes to your sleep hygiene, consider seeing your doctor to find out whether there are other things you can do to help yourself sleep better.

Even though your life is busy—full of fun and important activities—it's important to make room in your life for enough sleep. Sleep is like healthy food for your brain and body. Sleep nourishes and restores you, allowing you to be at your best. Your life is stressful enough; you don't need sleep deprivation adding to your difficulties. And you don't have to allow stress to get in the way of your sleep. Take good care of your sleep, and your sleep will take good care of you.

✳ Part 3 ✳

Your Life Journey

Chapter 17

Self-Compassion Means Taking Care of Yourself

Friendship with one's self is all important, because without it, one cannot be friends with anyone else.

— thirty-second First Lady of the United States
Eleanor Roosevelt

Self-compassion is critical in mindfulness, because it allows you to stay present with yourself and accept yourself when you are experiencing stress and difficulties. Cultivating an attitude of self-compassion, discussed in chapter 3, is only the first step. When stress arises, it's important that you put self-compassion into action by doing some self-care. At such times, though, it can be hard to remember what to do or to summon enough motivation and energy to take action. That's why coming up with a self-care plan in advance can help, and that is the focus of this chapter.

✳ *Dale's Story*

Dale said he was dealing with a lot of stress from school and from arguments with other teens. He shared that before he started taking the mindfulness course, the way he normally dealt with stress was "to shut everybody and everything out." He would close his bedroom door and stay in his room all day, keeping his stress to himself and ruminating on his problems.

But Dale had now begun to observe and learn more about his own stress and his reactions to stress. He had seen for himself how his habit of shutting out the world usually just made his stress worse: the longer he stayed by himself in his room, the more lonely and angry he felt. As he became more mindful and aware of his own decisions and behaviors, he saw that he could make different choices.

"Now," Dale told us, "I'm dealing with stress a lot better, not as negatively as I used to. Now I'm more [aware] of my triggers, and I'm able to avoid some of them. Also, now I tell my parents instead of just keeping everything to myself. That helps me feel better."

Know the Signs That You Are Getting Stressed

Certain changes in your body, in your mood, in your thoughts, and in your behaviors are "stress signatures"—signs that stress might be building up and starting to affect your physical and mental health. If you don't know the warning signs, stress can sneak up on you. The good news is you can practice becoming more aware of your stress signatures. Once you learn to recognize your stress signatures, you can take action to keep the stress from overwhelming you.

Download and print the "My Stress Signatures" worksheet from http://www.newharbinger.com/30802, and use it to help you identify your own stress signatures from the following list.

* Hopelessness

* Increased irritability and arguing

* Impatience and decreased politeness

* Sleep disturbance

* Physical pain or uncomfortable sensations (e.g., stomachache, headache, muscle tension, tightness in chest)

* Change in appetite

* Change in eating habits (e.g., eating too much or skipping meals)

* Decreased energy

* Decreased social contact/increased isolation

* Quitting or skipping a healthy activity (e.g., exercise)

* Decreased concentration

* Poor memory

* Increased guilt and sense of worthlessness

* Not dealing with usual stuff like hygiene or homework

* Poor judgment

* Increased procrastination

* Increased negative thoughts and rumination

* Apathy

* Agitation and anxiety

* Decreased ability to have fun or enjoy things

* Thoughts of self-harm

* Sadness and crying

* Increased use of substances (e.g., alcohol, marijuana)

If any stress signatures of yours aren't listed, write them in the blanks. Then write what, if anything, has prevented you from noticing and attending to these signs of stress in the past (for example, denial, self-medicating, blaming, arguments). Finally, name one or two people who can help you notice these signs of stress in the future. These are trusted people (for example, parents, friends, teachers, or coaches) you can ask to be on the lookout for your stress signatures, so that they can let you know when you seem stressed. A "stress early warning system" of supportive people can help you recognize what's happening earlier and start taking care of yourself sooner, because sometimes it's hard for you to see it yourself when stress is building up.

Self-Care in Action: Create Your Action Plan

When you recognize that stress is building up, the next step is to make a mindful choice to take care of yourself. The challenge is that when your lizard brain is activated, it's really hard to remember what to do! A Mindfulness and Resilience Action Plan (discussed next) and a Stress Management Emergency Plan can help remind you what to do when you get stressed.

You can personalize the Mindfulness and Resilience Action Plan available at http://www.newharbinger.com/30802, or you can make your own.

The first step in your Mindfulness and Resilience Action Plan should be to mindfully STOP, then practice the SOBER Breathing Space. Any time you are stressed out, it's critical to stop what you are doing, take a few breaths, and avoid acting out of stress. When you stop and come back to the present moment, you can choose a more mindful response (remember, the "R" in SOBER stands for "respond").

The second step is to do an activity that brings you a sense of pleasure or mastery. On your plan, under "Pleasure

Activities," list some things that you enjoy that are healthy for you—for example, listening to or playing music, walking your dog, painting or drawing, exercising or playing sports, and talking to a friend. Under "Mastery Activities," list some healthy behaviors that give you some sense of achievement, satisfaction, or control. Examples of Mastery Activities are cleaning your room, getting dressed, organizing your desk, writing down a list of things that you need to do, doing chores, doing homework, returning e-mails, and preparing a meal or snack. (Note that some activities can fit under both pleasure and mastery.) Any time you are stressed, after mindfully STOPping, try doing at least one activity from your list—even if you don't feel like it at that moment, and even if you don't believe that it would help. You might find that afterward, you don't feel as stressed or are in a better mood.

The third step is about making sure you are attending to four basic human needs: sleep, nutrition, exercise and activity, and social connectedness. Any time you are sleepy, hungry, restless, or lonely, it is much harder for your brain and body to handle stress. Simply seeing "sleep," "nutrition," "exercise and activity," and "social connectedness" listed in your plan may be all you need to remind yourself of this. Then, if you remember you missed breakfast or lunch, you can have a healthy snack. If you realize you're sick of sitting still, you can get up and do something active. If you've been isolating yourself, you can talk to someone or spend time with people you feel close to. If you realize you're exhausted and sleep-deprived, you can boost your alertness and energy with a ten-to-twenty-minute "power nap." To take a power nap, set an alarm on your phone for ten or twenty minutes. Lie down, or sit in a chair with your head leaning against a wall. Close your eyes and allow your body to rest without doing anything else. It doesn't matter if you actually fall asleep or not.

The fourth step is to practice one of the formal mindfulness skills that you've learned in this book. If you are using the Mindfulness and Resilience Action Plan from the website, circle one or two formal mindfulness practices that you've found helpful. Or choose from sitting meditation, belly breathing, walking meditation, mindful stretching, and the body scan.

The fifth step involves practicing informal mindfulness. On your Mindfulness and Resilience Action Plan, write down some activities that you enjoy incorporating mindfulness into, such as eating, writing, and playing music. Then write down any other actions that you might wish to take that would help you take care of yourself in moments of stress.

Keep a copy of your plan somewhere you can find it easily—for example, on your bedroom wall, in your backpack, on your computer desktop, or in your top desk drawer. When you notice your stress signatures arising, look at your plan and take action. Pick at least one action and do it as best you can—even if you don't feel like in that moment—knowing that your behaviors affect your mood. If you have time, take good care of yourself by practicing all five steps of your action plan. There might be situations where you don't have enough time to practice all five steps. In that case, practice step 1 (the STOP and SOBER practices), and then choose one or two other self-care actions from your list that you can do in that moment. Either way, be sure to congratulate yourself for any large or small action that you took, even if it wasn't the complete plan. Taking compassionate action to take care of yourself during times of stress will increase your resilience, so that you will be less likely to become overwhelmed by stress.

Have a Stress Management Emergency Plan

Sometimes when your stress is intense or overwhelming, you might not be able to find or execute your Mindfulness and Resilience Action Plan quickly enough. In those situations, It can be helpful to have a shorter and simpler plan that you can access anytime, anywhere: a Stress Management Emergency Plan.

You can download wallet-sized Stress Management Emergency Plan cards from http://www.newharbinger .com/30802 and print them out, or you can make your own.

Your Stress Management Emergency Plan starts with the SOBER Breathing Space. The Emergency Plan card reminds you of the steps in the SOBER practice (Stop, Observe, Breathe, Expand, Respond). The next step is to do some mindfulness and self-care activities. If you printed the cards from the website, circle two or three activities that often help you feel better, and add any other activities you can think of. Or choose from belly breathing, eating or drinking, talking, journaling, walking or exercising, and showering. The last step, if you are still feeling overwhelmed or unsafe, is to ask for help from a friend or a trusted adult (like a parent, an aunt or uncle, a teacher, or a coach). You can also call 1-800-273-TALK (in the United States) or visit the National Suicide Prevention Lifeline website (http://www.suicidepreventionlifeline.org), call 1-800-668-6868 (in Canada) or visit the Kids Help Phone website (http://www.kidshelpphone.ca), call 911, or go to a hospital emergency room. On your Stress Management Emergency Plan card, write down the person or number you would call.

Keep this card in your wallet, your purse, your backpack, or your cell phone or mobile device (that is, take a picture of it). The next time you are experiencing intense or overwhelming stress, don't panic. Remember that you have powerful tools to handle even intense stress. Look at your Stress Management Emergency Plan, as a reminder from yourself. Read it in a voice of compassion. Then, act on your plan with as much mindfulness and self-compassion as you can.

✲ *Ronald's Story*

Ronald was a creative and sensitive young man who loved sports and loved to laugh, but his anger had gotten him into some trouble at school and at home. He said that he had a tendency to get angry at the people around him whenever he was stressed.

For example, one week he told the class, "I was really angry this week at this kid at my school. I was so choked. But I knew I was angry—I was aware of it. Maybe I should have meditated. But I couldn't sit down to meditate; I was too upset for that. So instead I went and worked out."

I told Ronald, "It sounds like you actually were being mindful, even if you didn't mean to be! First of all, you recognized that you were angry, in that moment. Secondly, you made a mindful choice to do something to take care of yourself, instead of acting on your anger. And, thirdly, maybe instead of formal sitting meditation, your mindfulness practice is 'working out meditation.' As long as you're aware, that's mindfulness!"

Self-Care Isn't Selfish

If you were to study the anatomy of the human heart, you would learn that the heart pumps blood to itself first, before it pumps blood to the rest of your body. In other words, in order to take care of your body, your heart needs to take care of itself first. Perhaps you can take a lesson from your own heart. It's crucial (and not at all selfish) to learn to take care of yourself first, before you can take care of others.

Self-care is about becoming your own best friend. Once you can be a better friend to yourself, you can be a better friend to others. If you don't know how to care for your own stress, you can't offer as much to other people when they are stressed. So, loving-kindness and self-compassion are really just two sides of the same coin.

You deserve to take care of yourself, especially when you are stressed. Noticing your own signs of stress is a practice in awareness. Taking care of yourself is mindfulness in action.

Chapter 18

Putting Your Life on a Mindful Path

You are perfect the way you are...and
you could use a little improvement.

— Zen Master Shunryu Suzuki Roshi

Congratulations on having taken your first steps down
the path of mindfulness. Take a moment to reflect on your
experiences so far:

* What were your intentions when you first started
  experimenting with mindfulness?

* What benefits have you experienced from
  mindfulness practice?

* Would you like to continue practicing mindfulness?
  If so, why?

* What has gotten in the way of your practice of mindfulness and of being more present in your daily life?

* What would help you continue to practice and to live more mindfully?

Now, let's explore how you can maintain and continue your mindfulness practice. I hope that the end of this book won't be the end of your mindful journey, but rather only the beginning.

Teen Voices: *Nicole R.*

"After my mindfulness group was over, I did not want my mindfulness journey to end. I had seen the benefits and wanted to continue to incorporate mindfulness into my life. This was not easy, though. Finding time for mindfulness between my choir rehearsals, [my] soccer practices, and my first year of university was very difficult.

"At home, I would practice mindfulness in the more formal way. I would do sitting meditation when I got home from school or just before bed to help me sleep. I found that taking time out of my day to calm my mind and focus on my breathing was extremely grounding. As a teen [and] young adult, sometimes it is very hard to find those small moments to just let things stop and enjoy something as simple as a breath. This part of my practice was, and still is, my favorite.

"At school, I would practice SOBER breathing and remind myself to stop and breathe from time to time. Instead of racing through my schoolwork, I tried to take time to really appreciate and enjoy what I was learning. Approaching my work this way, rather than as something I had to race through, actually gave me a greater appreciation for what I was learning, and I found it much easier to apply the content to my everyday life. In addition, doing some breathing before tests really helped calm any anxieties that I had. I also reminded myself throughout the day to just take things one day at a time, focus on what had to be done today, and leave tomorrow for tomorrow.

"When my anxiety got overwhelming, I would go to a quiet place and ground myself. I would practice my breathing, smile to myself, and not judge myself on how I was feeling. I'd just allow my thoughts to float through my head like clouds and focus on the rhythm of my breath until I felt calm again. Then I would continue with my day, always with a smile."

Radical Acceptance and the Art of Mindful Living

As you've learned by now, mindfulness can be a powerful tool to handle stress. But, it can also be much more than just a "trick" or "technique" to do when you're stressed. At its heart, mindfulness is a way of being, a way of seeing, and a way of relating to yourself and to others that can transform your life, your family, and your community.

Choosing to live mindfully is an act of real courage. It may often mean going against the grain. Our society bombards us with the message that in order to be happy, we always have to do more, be more, buy more, and get more. Advertisements, for example, try to convince you that you are never good enough or smart enough, you don't own enough cool stuff, and you're not beautiful enough. These messages can cause a huge amount of stress.

Living mindfully means liberating yourself from these messages, by radically accepting who you are and what you already have, right here and now. Psychologist and meditation teacher Tara Brach writes about the liberating power of radical acceptance: "When we put down ideas of what life *should* be like, we are free to wholeheartedly say yes to our life as it is" (2003, 86, my italics). You don't need more possessions or achievements or awards. You are already complete—and beautiful—just as you are.

Radical acceptance isn't the same thing as indifference. It doesn't mean saying, "Whatever. Who cares?" when you are faced with difficulties. Instead, it means becoming intimate with both your joys *and* your difficulties, with complete acceptance, while at the same time not getting carried away by any of it. From this place of openness, you can awaken your inner wisdom and allow it to flow through you. In this way, everything that you say and do can arise from your innate wisdom and compassion.

Bird in the Hand: Maintaining Your Practice

When I first started practicing mindfulness, after my first three-week meditation retreat, I came home really motivated and enthusiastic to continue meditating. For the first few weeks, I enjoyed my daily sitting meditation, and it helped me get through my day with less stress. But, after a few weeks, my old automatic pilot habits came back. I started thinking that I was too busy or too tired to meditate, or that I had more important things to do.

Since then, I've gone through many ups and downs in my mindfulness practice. There are definitely times when I'd rather distract myself with things that don't really matter, like checking my social networking sites for the tenth time that day. One thing I've observed, however, is that my life is almost always better when I practice more regularly. At the same time, I know from experience how difficult it can be to keep practicing regularly when life gets busy.

An old Zen Master said that maintaining a regular mindfulness practice is like holding a delicate bird in your hands. If you try too hard to hold onto it, you might injure the bird. On the other hand, if you're too laid-back about holding onto it, the bird will fly away! Maintaining a mindfulness practice is kind of like holding that bird: you need a firm intention and commitment and, at the same time, a soft and gentle touch.

On the one hand, we all have a tendency to *not* stay present— to go through our day on autopilot, to seek distractions. So, it does take some intention and self-discipline to continually train yourself in the art of living mindfully, to stay present, and to practice every day or every week. I don't mean the kind of self-discipline where you force yourself to do something you don't want to do. I'm talking about a gentle effort, born from your own experience of the benefits of mindfulness.

At the same time, it's important not to make your mindfulness practice a source of stress, or another expectation to judge yourself against. Mindfulness practice shouldn't feel like hard work. You don't need to try to achieve some goal, even something like becoming less stressed or being more relaxed or happy. Happiness and peace are already inside of you. When you stop reaching for them, they are more likely to emerge on their own. So, just practice being present with yourself, simply for the sake of being present—simply for the sake of being truly alive.

Someone once asked Vietnamese Zen Master Thich Nhat Hanh, "How do you know whether you are practicing mindfulness correctly?" To which he answered, "If you are enjoying the practice, if it is bringing you more peace and happiness, then you know that you are practicing correctly." So, trust your intuitive wisdom and enjoy the practice—each breath and each step.

Everyone encounters obstacles on the path of mindfulness. In fact, you can learn a lot about yourself simply by examining—with acceptance and nonjudgment—your habits and your tendencies to *not* be present. For example, if you are planning to meditate, but you have a thought like *I don't feel like meditating right now* or *I'd rather check my phone,* just take a moment to observe that urge. You don't need to fight or judge it. Be compassionately aware of your resistance, breathing with it. The more you observe, the more clearly you will see how some of your tendencies and behaviors don't serve you very well or only make you more stressed out. As your self-compassion grows, the more you will simply love yourself so much that you won't want to make yourself suffer anymore.

──────────Teen Voices: *Nicole R.*──────────

"If you can...join a mindfulness group or club. I find that having people to practice with and to support you makes your mindfulness practice easier and much more rewarding."

Tips for Maintaining a Mindfulness Practice

Here are some tips to help you continue a daily mindfulness practice.

* Use mindfulness apps on your phone or mobile device.
    Check out the "Resources" at http://www .newharbinger.com/30802 for the names of a few apps.

* Schedule and practice a short daily meditation (for example, sitting meditation or the body scan) at the same time every day.

I've found it more helpful to meditate a little bit every day, even just for two to five minutes, than to meditate for longer periods but less often. As best you can, meditate just because you've decided to—just because it's time to meditate—even if you don't feel like it at that exact moment. I've had to overcome my own resistance to meditating many, many times, and not once have I thought afterward, *Wow, that was a waste. I wish I hadn't meditated!*

✱ Set a reminder on your cell phone for your daily meditation.

✱ Get a meditation bell for your home.
   A simple chime from a music store, or an Asian-style meditation bell (see the "Resources" at http://www.newharbinger.com/30802), can enrich your practice at home. Simply ringing the bell and breathing mindfully three times in the morning and at night can help relieve stress.

✱ Find some friends along the path.
   It can be difficult to meditate by yourself. So, invite a friend or family member to try meditation with you. You can do a simple practice like listening to the bell, or you can try a guided meditation. If your friend or family member enjoys the experience, invite him or her to practice meditation with you once a week or once a month. You can even invite a third person, or start a small mindfulness club or group. Start each meeting

with one or two formal meditations, like the body scan, sitting meditation, or walking meditation. Then, perhaps enjoy a mindful meal and mindful conversation together, sharing your joys and challenges in living mindfully, and creating brotherhood or sisterhood together.

* Schedule a "Lazy Day" (Nhat Hanh 2009) once a week or once a month.

    Instead of doing something all the time, taking some time to "do nothing" can be very nourishing. Downtime gives your body and brain a chance to recover from chronic stress. Give yourself a day to let go of homework, jobs, and projects. Start the day with a body scan or sitting meditation. Then, let the rest of the day unfold naturally and playfully, with relaxing and enjoyable activities. For example, you might wish to go on a walk or play with your younger cousin. If you have the opportunity, spending time in nature can be very healing. Breathe mindfully, stay present, and appreciate the little moments that you sometimes take for granted.

* Invent new ways of practicing the SOBER Breathing Space, adapting it to the situation.

    If you don't have time to practice a full three-minute SOBER Breathing Space, experiment with practicing it for just one minute. Experiment with the SOBER Breathing Space in different situations in your life, such as when you arrive at school or sit down for class. Practice it as a way to shift out of

217

autopilot, free yourself from stressful rumination, and reenter the situation with mindful clarity and compassion.

* Invent new informal mindfulness practices.
    In a lighthearted spirit of experimentation, for one week, see whether you can find a new activity every day to use as a way of practicing informal mindfulness.

* Use all your senses.
    Instead of trying to tune out noise and other distractions while you're meditating, tune in to your surroundings, with mindful intention. Experiment with "listening meditation," "seeing meditation," "feeling meditation," and "smelling meditation."

* Invent your own mindfulness phrases.
    Whatever is happening around you and within you, you can breathe with it and smile to it. Invent your own short phrases to remind you to breathe mindfully and stay present in stressful situations with curiosity and kindness. For example, *Little brother annoying me—breathing*. Or *Hello, test anxiety—smiling to you*. Or *Breathing in, aware of stress in my body. Breathing out, letting go.*

* Place reminders and inspirations in your environment.
    I have a large piece of calligraphy by Thich Nhat Hanh mounted on my wall at home. It says

"Breathe." Every time I see it, it reminds me to breathe and smile mindfully. Artwork like this can inspire you on your mindful journey. Phrases, quotes (such as those at the beginning of each chapter), and poems can remind you to stay present. Find some you like, write them in your own handwriting, and put them on your wall.

* Go on a mindfulness retreat.

    Going on a mindfulness retreat for a few days can be a life-changing chance to immerse yourself fully in the practice and truly experience a different way of being. See the "Resources" at http://www .newharbinger.com/30802 for mindfulness retreats for teens and families.

* Get connected to mindfulness on social networking sites.

    Like "The Mindful Teen" on Facebook and follow @TheMindfulTeen on Twitter. Check out the "Resources" link at http://www.newharbinger .com/30802 for other mindfulness-related web pages. You can also create your own online group among your mindful friends, so that you can share your experiences and inspiration with one another.

* Be gentle with yourself.

    Don't get too attached to expectations about what meditation is supposed to be like or what it is supposed to do for you. Mindfulness is a journey, not a destination or an outcome. If you think, *It's not working* or *I must be doing it wrong*, simply notice those thoughts arising and falling away, without taking them to be true. Remember that thoughts are just thoughts; thoughts are not facts. And don't be too hard on yourself. If you don't meditate as often as you might, or if you skip one of your regular meditation times, that's okay.

✱ Return to your mindfulness practice.

Even if you forget to practice mindfulness for a long time, or if you get too busy to meditate, the present moment is always there for you, inviting you to return. You don't need to regret not having practiced for a week, a month, or even a year. You don't need to judge yourself for it, either. Mindfulness is very forgiving. Every moment is an invitation to start over.

Your Mindfulness Practice Plan

For this section, you can personalize the Mindfulness Practice Plan available at http://www.newharbinger.com/30802, or you can make your own.

In the first section, "My Vision and Intentions," write down your vision and intentions. Why would you want to continue a mindfulness practice? How might a mindfulness practice help you specifically? For example, might it help you manage your stress, help you manage your anger, help you in school, or help you manage your pain? Think of the unique situations and challenges you face. This will help motivate you on your path.

In the second section, "Formal Practices That I Want to Make Time For," make note of any formal mindfulness practices (sitting meditation, belly breathing, walking meditation, loving-kindness meditation, the body scan) that you want to continue. Write down how many minutes per day and how often you would like to practice them. Make a note of the specific days. This can help you make formal mindfulness practice part of your everyday routine.

In the third section, "Informal Practices That I Want to Make a Part of My Everyday Life," note what kinds of informal mindfulness practices you'd like to make a part of your life—for example, bells of mindfulness, mindfulness of your pain, mindful writing or walking, mindful eating, mindful STOPping, mindfulness of your thoughts, the SOBER Breathing Space, mindfully petting your dog or cat, mindful listening, mindfulness of your feelings, and mindful speaking. You can also identify "bells of mindfulness"—ways to remind yourself to be mindful as you go about your day—for example, by setting reminders on your phone or using a mindfulness app every day.

Keep a copy of your Mindfulness Practice Plan in a place where you will see it often, to remind you of how you want to practice. For example, tape it to your bedroom wall or door, or save it as a photo on your cell phone or computer. Review it once a week to remember and strengthen your mindful intention. Be gentle with yourself; think of this plan as more of a reminder and an invitation than an expectation or assignment.

In a month or so, revise your Mindfulness Practice Plan, based on your actual experience with mindfulness in your daily life.

A Final Word: Making the Practice Your Own

Don't simply believe anything I've said in this book. And don't believe anything that anyone else has told you about mindfulness, either—instead, try it and see for yourself. Your mindfulness practice is all about you—learning from your own experience and observations about your own mind, your own body, and your own life. You are your own teacher, your own expert, your own guide. To develop your mindfulness practice, take what you've learned in this book and then apply what works for you in your own life. Only then you can discover how mindfulness can help you find strength you didn't know you had.

I hope this is just the beginning of your mindful journey, not the end. Life is too short and too precious to go through it on autopilot. Don't wait to start living your life! The wisdom and strength that you can cultivate through the art of mindful living will serve you well for the rest of your life, if you let it. The more you are there for your mindfulness practice, the more your mindfulness will be there for you. I wish you the best, and I know that you can succeed. May you be happy, may you be free from stress, and may you and all beings be at peace.

Resources

The Mindful Teen Online

New Harbinger Publications' *Mindful Teen* **web page.** This web page provides the downloadables (see below) for use with *The Mindful Teen*. It also hosts a list of apps, websites, books, and other resources for teens and their families who wish to learn and practice mindfulness.

http://www.newharbinger.com/30802

Facebook. Like "The Mindful Teen" on Facebook to receive regular inspirational quotes, poems, and articles to help you keep your mindfulness practice fresh and alive.

http://www.facebook.com/themindfulteen

Twitter. Follow The Mindful Teen (@TheMindfulTeen) for mindful tweets!

https://twitter.com/themindfulteen

MindfulnessforTeens.com. This website, created by *The Mindful Teen* author Dzung Vo, contains more information, meditations, videos, and resources on mindfulness for teens.

Downloadable Accessories

Guided Meditations

1. Eating a Raisin Mindfully (~5 min) (chapter 2)

2. Mindful Breathing (~5 min) (chapter 2)

3. Sitting Meditation (~10 min) (chapter 4)

4. Body Scan (Short) (~5 min) (chapter 6)

5. SOBER Breathing Space (~3 min) (chapter 7)

6. Walking Meditation (~5 min) (chapter 8)

7. Mindful Movement (~10 min) (chapter 8)

8. Mindfulness of Thinking (~5 min) (chapter 9)

9. SOBER Coping Space (Handling a Difficulty) (~3 min) (chapter 10)

10. Loving-Kindness Meditation (~5 min) (chapter 12)

11. Body Scan (Long) (~30 min) (chapter 16)

Worksheet and Plans

My Stress Signatures (chapter 17)

My Mindfulness and Resilience Action Plan (chapter 17)

My Stress Management Emergency Plan (chapter 17)

My Mindfulness Practice Plan (chapter 18)

Further Reading

Gina M. Biegel, *The Stress Reduction Workbook for Teens: Mindfulness Skills to Help You Deal with Stress* (New Harbinger Publications, 2009)

Joseph V. Ciarrochi, Louise Hayes, and Ann Bailey, *Get Out of Your Mind and Into Your Life for Teens: A Guide to Living an Extraordinary Life* (New Harbinger Publications, 2012)

Thich Nhat Hanh, *Happiness: Essential Mindfulness Practices* (Parallax Press, 2009)

Mark C. Purcell and Jason R. Murphy, *Mindfulness for Teen Anger: A Workbook to Overcome Anger and Aggression Using MBSR and DBT Skills* (New Harbinger Publications, 2014)

Bob Stahl and Elisha Goldstein, *A Mindfulness-Based Stress Reduction Workbook* (New Harbinger Publications, 2010)

Christopher Willard, *Mindfulness for Teen Anxiety: A Workbook for Overcoming Anxiety at Home, at School, and Everywhere Else* (New Harbinger Publications, 2014)

Mark Williams, John Teasdale, Zindel Segal, and Jon Kabat-Zinn, *The Mindful Way Through Depression: Freeing Yourself from Chronic Unhappiness* (Guilford Press, 2007)

References

American Academy of Pediatrics. 2014. "Let Them Sleep: AAP Recommends Delaying Start Times of Middle and High Schools to Combat Teen Sleep Deprivation." Press release, August 25. http://www.aap.org/en-us/about-the-aap/aap-press-room/Pages/Let -Them-Sleep-AAP-Recommends-Delaying-Start-Times-of-Middle -and-High-Schools-to-Combat-Teen-Sleep-Deprivation.aspx.

Baraz, James. 2007. *Awakening Joy*. Online course. http://www.awak eningjoy.info.

Biegel, Gina M. 2009. *The Stress Reduction Workbook for Teens: Mindfulness Skills to Help You Deal with Stress*. Oakland, CA: New Harbinger Publications.

Biegel, Gina M., Kirk W. Brown, Shauna L. Shapiro, and Christine M. Schubert. 2009. "Mindfulness-Based Stress Reduction for the Treatment of Adolescent Psychiatric Outpatients: A Randomized Clinical Trial." *Journal of Consulting and Clinical Psychology* 77: 855–66.

Bowen, Sarah, Neha Chawla, and G. Alan Marlatt. 2011. *Mindfulness-Based Relapse Prevention for Addictive Behaviors: A Clinician's Guide*. New York: Guilford Press.

Brach, Tara. 2003. *Radical Acceptance: Embracing Your Life with the Heart of a Buddha*. New York: Bantam.

Chödrön, Pema. 1996. *Awakening Loving-Kindness*. Boston: Shambhala.

Fox, Michael J. 2007. "What I've Learned: Michael J. Fox." By Scott Raab. *Esquire*, December 17. http://www.esquire.com/features /what-ive-learned/michaeljfox0108.

Hancock, Herbie. 2010. "Musical Legend Herbie Hancock Fuses Jazz, Global Rhythms." Interview by Jeffrey Brown. *NewsHour*, PBS, September 16. Available at http://www.pbs.org/newshour/bb /entertainment/july-dec10/herbie_09-16.html.

Hayes, Stephen C., Kirk D. Strosahl, and Kelly G. Wilson. 1999. *Acceptance and Commitment Therapy: An Experiential Approach to Behavior Change*. New York: Guilford Press.

Hollon, Steven D., and Philip C. Kendall. 1980. "Cognitive Self-Statements in Depression: Development of an Automatic Thoughts Questionnaire." *Cognitive Therapy and Research* 4: 383–95.

Kabat-Zinn, Jon. 1994. *Wherever You Go, There You Are: Mindfulness Meditation in Everyday Life*. New York: Hyperion.

———. 2012. "Q&A: Jon Kabat-Zinn Talks About Bringing Mindfulness Meditation to Medicine." By Maia Szalavitz. *Time*, January 11. http://healthland.time.com/2012/01/11/mind-reading-jon-kabat -zinn-talks-about-bringing-mindfulness-meditation-to-medicine.

———. 2013. *Full Catastrophe Living: Using the Wisdom of Your Body and Mind to Face Stress, Pain, and Illness*. Rev. and updated ed. New York: Bantam Books.

Kelty Mental Health Resource Centre. 2011. *Healthy Living, Healthy Minds: A Toolkit for Health Professionals: Promoting Healthy Living in Children and Youth with Mental Health Challenges*. 2nd ed. Available at http://www.keltymentalhealth.ca/toolkit-families.

Lao-tzu. 2006. *Tao Te Ching: A New English Version* (reprint). Translated by Stephen Mitchell. New York: Harper Perennial Modern Classics.

Mumford, George. 2011. "Mindfulness and Basketball: An Interview with George Mumford." Blog entry by Soren Gordhamer. *Soren Gordhamer: Exploring Ancient Wisdom in Modern Life...* http://www.sorengordhamer.com/News/single_post/mindfulness-and-basketball-an-interview-with-george-mumford.

National Sleep Foundation. 2014. "How Much Sleep Do We Really Need?" http://sleepfoundation.org/how-sleep-works/how-much-sleep-do-we-really-need.

Nhat Hanh, Thich. 1990. *Present Moment Wonderful Moment: Mindfulness Verses for Daily Living.* Berkeley, CA: Parallax Press.

———. 1993. *The Blooming of a Lotus: Guided Meditation for Achieving the Miracle of Mindfulness.* Boston: Beacon Press.

———. 2001. *Anger: Wisdom for Cooling the Flames.* New York: Riverhead Books.

———. 2007. *The Art of Power.* New York: HarperOne.

———. 2009. *Happiness: Essential Mindfulness Practices.* Berkeley, CA: Parallax Press.

———. 2010. "Oprah Talks to Thich Nhat Hanh." Interview by Oprah Winfrey. *O, The Oprah Magazine,* March. Available at http://www.oprah.com/spirit/Oprah-Talks-to-Thich-Nhat-Hanh.

Pietzker, Mary Ann. 1872. "Is It True? Is It Necessary? Is It Kind?" *Miscellaneous Poems.* London: Griffith and Farran.

Segal, Zindel V., J. Mark G. Williams, and John D. Teasdale. 2013. *Mindfulness-Based Cognitive Therapy for Depression.* 2nd ed. New York: Guilford Press.

Siegel, Daniel J. 2010. *Mindsight: The New Science of Personal Transformation.* New York: Bantam Books.

Stahl, Bob, and Elisha Goldstein. 2010. *A Mindfulness-Based Stress Reduction Workbook.* Oakland, CA: New Harbinger Publications.

Sullivan, Walter. 1972. "The Einstein Papers: A Man of Many Parts." *New York Times*, March 29. Available from http://www.nytimes .com.

Swindoll, Charles R. 2009. "The Value of a Positive Attitude." January 20. http://daily.insight.org/site/News2?page=NewsArticle&#002 2;id=13123.

Dzung X. Vo, MD, FAAP, is a pediatrician specializing in adolescent medicine at British Columbia Children's Hospital, and clinical assistant professor at the University of British Columbia Faculty of Medicine, Vancouver, Canada. His medical practice, teaching, and research emphasize promoting resilience in young people to help them thrive in the face of complex stress and adversity. He has helped to develop and teach mindfulness training programs for youth with chronic stress, chronic pain, depression, and anxiety.

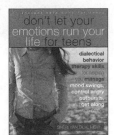

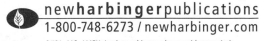

Register your **new harbinger** titles for additional benefits!

When you register your **new harbinger** title—purchased in any format, from any source—you get access to benefits like the following:

- Downloadable accessories like printable worksheets and extra content
- Instructional videos and audio files
- Information about updates, corrections, and new editions

Not every title has accessories, but we're adding new material all the time.

Access free accessories in 3 easy steps:

1. Sign in at NewHarbinger.com (or **register** to create an account).

2. Click on **register a book**. Search for your title and click the **register** button when it appears.

3. Click on the **book cover or title** to go to its details page. Click on **accessories** to view and access files.

That's all there is to it!

If you need help, visit:

NewHarbinger.com/accessories

new harbinger
CELEBRATING
40 YEARS